Are You Really Listening? thoughtfully treats essential, but often overlooked, social and relationship skills. From helping us develop a better ear for listening to teaching us how to constructively respond, the authors have created a first class approach to improving our ability to listen, and to be active relationship partners.

—Carter McClelland,
Chairman, Banc of America Securities

Drs. Donoghue and Siegel present clear and well-illustrated suggestions for active listening and sensitive responding to the thoughts expressed by others. The authors have captured the essence of those dry counseling textbook suggestions and framed them in an engaging, delightful context. In a user-friendly format *Are You Really Listening?* will be helpful to all who value and seek to enhance their interpersonal relationships.

—Donna MacNeill Heffner,
Certified School Psychologist

My profession as a bereavement counselor requires that I be a good listener. But what surprised me when I read this excellent book was the realization that I do not apply these skills, as I should, in my personal life!

—Janet Taylor, LCSW,
Center for Hope, Darien, Connecticut

Statistically, most of us will think we don't need a book to learn how to listen better—but we believe that others do because we don't feel heard. Donoghue and Siegel bring awareness to non-listening behaviors. We are often well intentioned but that is no substitute for effective listening. Their approach to listening creates teams in marriage, parenting, friendship, and at work. They demonstrate how we can genuinely enjoy our differences and strengthen any personal or professional relationship when we listen and are heard. In the process, we learn to be our best selves for others.

—The Very Reverend
Dr. James A. Kowalski, Dean,
The Cathedral of St. John the Divine,
New York, NY

Required reading for any professional. In practicing medicine, the coin of the realm is trust. Techniques of non-judgmental active listening are critical to its genesis. Donoghue and Siegel facilitate its acquisition by clear pertinent examples drawn from their own rich experience.

—Nicholas Kopeloff, M.D.
Greenwich, Connecticut

Reading Paul Donoghue's and Mary Siegel's book *Are You Really Listening?* was a great learning experience for me. These two experienced therapists make listening sound simple. I appreciated the wealth of knowledge and experience that the authors showed and I loved their down-to-earth examples. They convinced me that listening well to others is learning to love better. This is a book you will enjoy reading and love to keep.

—Sister Kathleen Kanet, RSHM
President, The Center of
International Learning
New York, NY

For the leader or manager, effective listening is a necessary skill. It helps to establish the kind of working relationships that get results. *Are You Really Listening?* describes the situations all of us encounter at work that are resolved only by good listening.

—J. Philip Bender,
Managing Partner, Northwestern Mutual
Financial Network

Are You Really *Listening?*

Keys to Successful Communication

PAUL J. DONOGHUE, Ph.D.
MARY E. SIEGEL, Ph.D.

SORIN BOOKS   Notre Dame, Indiana

PAUL J. DONOGHUE, Ph.D. and MARY E. SIEGEL, Ph.D. are psychologists in private practice in Stamford, Connecticut. They are also consultants to corporations and organizations in the United States, Canada, and Europe. Their work has been featured on CNBC and *Good Day New York*, *The Today Show*, and in *The New York Times*.

PAUL J. DONOGHUE

MARY E. SIEGEL

www.sorinbooks.com

ISBN-10 1-893732-88-6   ISBN-13 978-1-893732-88-9

Cover by John Carson

Text design by Katherine Robinson Coleman

Printed and bound in the United States of America.

Library of Congress Cataloging-in-Publication Data

Donoghue, Paul J.
  Are you really listening? : keys to successful communication / Paul J. Donoghue, Mary E. Siegel.
      p. cm.
  Includes bibliographical references.
  ISBN 1-893732-88-6 (pbk.)
  1. Listening. I. Siegel, Mary E. II. Title.

BF323.L5D66 2005
153.6'8—dc22

2005010036

Contents

To the Touchstone Team
who have taught and modeled listening
since 1970, starting with
the original team and Brenda Byrne
to the present team:
John Balistreri
Mark Driscoll
Carol Look
Dennis Shaughnessy
Rita Shaughnessy
Matthew Siegel
Suzanne Sperry

We would like to thank

John Balistreri, Carol Look, and Joan Conlin

for their patient proofreading and editing.

We would also like to thank our editor at

Sorin Books, Catherine M. Odell,

for her valuable editorial suggestions.

FOREWORD

What a better world it would be if we were all listening to each other!

I am required every day in my professional work and in my home life as a wife and as a mother to listen effectively. I learned early in my career as a television journalist, particularly as co-host of *Good Morning America*, that listening is the key to being a good interviewer as well as to being an effective collaborator with colleagues. I realized that the more I listened, the more the people I interviewed would open up, offering their candid views and experiences.

I too have been interviewed many times as an author of several books, including my most recent book, *Growing Up Healthy*. When I felt I was genuinely heard by the interviewer, I then felt ready to open up and talk. When the interviewer expressed respect, interest, and an understanding of my thoughts—rather than busily preparing his or her own thought or the next question—I had the opportunity and space to clarify and develop the point that I was making.

While listening is imperative in the working world, nowhere is it more important than in one's home life. As a parent watching my children grow and learn, I realize every day the paramount importance of listening. I also understand the value of always listening carefully to my husband and soulmate Jeff. This is particularly crucial when we are making decisions regarding our family and home.

I also find it easier to open up and express my true feelings when I feel that I am being heard. And of course as a parent, listening is always crucial—from our babies' first cries, to our toddlers' first attempts to verbalize their feelings, to our teenagers' need to be heard. Listening is undeniably one of the greatest gifts we can bestow upon our children.

While all of us want to be good listeners, in Are You Really Listening?, Doctors Donoghue and Siegel offer a valuable road map to the art of listening. The authors remind us with all-too-recognizable examples of the ways that we don't listen. They have created a simple step-by-step guide on how to be better listeners. I found Are You Really Listening? refreshing, eye-opening, and immensely helpful for my daily life. I trust that you will too.

Joan Lunden
author and former television co-host
of *Good Morning America*

PART ONE

Is *Anybody* Listening?

They would not listen.
They did not know how.

—*"Vincent" by Don McLean*

CHAPTER ONE

The
Importance
of
Listening

People don't listen. It's a universal complaint. Parents bewail the fact that their children don't listen; children are convinced that their parents don't even try to hear them. Wives are desperate for their husbands' attention while husbands give up trying to be heard by their wives. Bosses are certain that those working for them don't listen; employees won't speak up, sure that the boss doesn't want to hear. Patients can't get their doctors to concentrate on what they are saying. Doctors have the identical complaint about their patients. Everyone wants to be understood, but few people feel that they are. Surprisingly, most people think that they are good listeners.

What's going on here? Half of the population complains that the other half isn't listening while the half being accused are themselves complaining that they are not heard. When we ask audiences at our lectures if they think they are poor listeners, only a few people hesitantly raise their hands. The majority of these folks sits complacently until, one by one, they're nudged by a partner or child sitting nearby. We can admit that we don't play golf well or don't have a good memory, but we fail to admit that we listen poorly. We don't even know it, let alone admit it.

Before we can learn to listen, it is necessary to heighten awareness that in many instances and with many people *we do not listen.*

First of all, we don't listen when given information. Children play a game called "Telephone" that demonstrates this phenomenon of non-listening. One child whispers information to a playmate and tells her to pass it on until it reaches the last person in a row or circle. It always startles and amuses everyone in the group when they recognize how distorted the information is by the time it reaches the last person. The final report is always quite different from the original.

Most of us are not much better at the "Telephone" game. Assuming that we are attentive listeners—even when the message is trivial or mundane—is a misconception. For

We can admit that we don't play golf well or don't have a good memory, but we fail to admit that we listen poorly. We don't even know it, let alone admit it.

example, we ask for directions, close the car window, and then can't recall whether we should go left or right at the third light. Maybe we were distracted by our embarrassment at having to ask directions. Maybe we just weren't paying attention.

We do pay attention when people are talking about us. But ironically, that attention doesn't improve our ability to listen clearly. In our need to be liked, and affirmed, we stay attuned to any remark that might relate to us. If a teacher hears one of her students say, "I'm bored with math," she may "hear" a student complaining that she is a boring teacher. The student might well be talking about himself—his failure to understand the subject or his lack of aptitude in math. He might even be referring obliquely to problems that have nothing to do with math. Perhaps he is wounded by a lack of friends or by problems at home. The teacher, however, assumes that this negative assessment about math class is all about her.

A wife might say that she is worried about not feeling more sexual passion. Her husband could easily "hear" that she is not finding him attractive or that she is bored with the way he makes love.

This kind of listening—or rather non-listening behavior—that concludes that the speaker's message is "about me" is a form of selective attention. A speaker might be making several points, but the message that refers to us is often the only part that sparks our interest.

For example, Lorna comes home from work and tells her roommate, Samantha,

I had a nightmare of a day! I accidentally erased that entire report I had been working on for next week's staff meeting from the computer. I was out of my mind with worry. Thank God, Mitch was able to retrieve it. But, then Donna e-mailed me to tell me that it wasn't a good time to give the report. That confusion took even more time and e-mailing to straighten out. Finally at the end of the day, my car wouldn't start because the battery was dead. Some nice guy from accounting jumped it for me.

Samantha selectively hears the part of Lorna's "tale of woe" that interests her. "I hope the battery is OK now, " she responds. "Remember, you're lending the car to me this weekend to move stuff on Saturday." Selective attention keeps us from hearing all that the speaker is trying to communicate. We hear not what is important to the speaker but what matters most to us.

We listen even less adequately when we are subjected to threatening messages. Any remark that sounds critical about our looks, dress, pronunciation, or performance is often almost impossible for us to hear.

Conversely and strangely, words of praise or compliments can conflict with our own self-image, causing such suspicion or discomfort that they are quickly brushed aside. We rebuff or can't "hear" compliments. Kate describes a painful instance of such a dismissal:

> *I watched Nickie, a friend of mine, help her elderly mother get into the car after Mass one Sunday. Nickie seemed so gentle, holding her mother's hand until she was in the car and tucking her coat in around her legs. When I told her that I thought she was so sweet and kind to her mother, Nickie said, "Oh, Kate, you always think everybody is nice." I was so hurt and insulted. I felt foolish for telling her my thoughts.*

We hear not what is important to the speaker but what matters most to us.

Nickie may have felt awkward at being complimented, or even guilty because she really wasn't feeling kindly toward her mother. Whatever she was feeling, she wasn't able to hear Kate.

So many of us are also likely to rebut or reject statements that contradict our own views. In fact, we tend to prepare to do verbal battle even before we understand what someone else has said. We will become good listeners only when we can acknowledge that we have a lot to learn.

> We will become good listeners only when we can acknowledge that we have a lot to learn.

We Need to Be Heard

Becoming more aware of our listening hurdles can start with reflections on our own need to be heard. How deeply rewarding it is when we are understood. Carl Rogers, the wise humanistic psychologist, spoke of the soothing effect of being heard by :

> . . . individuals who have heard me without judging me, diagnosing me, appraising me, evaluating me. They have just listened and clarified and responded to me at all the levels at which I was communicating. . . . When I have been listened to and when I have been heard, I am able to re-perceive my world in a new way and to go on. It is astonishing how elements which seem insoluble become soluble when someone listens.

It is rewarding to be heard accurately, but it is frustrating and painful when we are not. This young couple endured the painful consequences of misunderstanding:

Jenna and Scott sat in their car in stony silence. Then he said, "I don't get what I did wrong. I just said you looked sexy in that dress." Jenna spat back, "But you said it in front of everyone—even your nephew. That was so inappropriate. It's like you were slobbering over me in front of your whole family. It was so embarrassing. Your mother probably thinks we are sleeping together now."

Jenna experienced humiliation and anxiety in this misreading of Scott's attention and comments. She didn't hear his pride in her, or his delight in her appearance. So, she derived no pleasure from the statement Scott intended as a genuine compliment. Later, Jenna couldn't understand or accept Scott's explanation, and she responded again with an angry accusation.

Listening Liberates

In contrast to the sad result of Scott and Jenna's miscommunication, we recently witnessed the comfort provided by a father's tender listening. At a ski slope, we watched a father greet his son who had just finished last in a slalom race. The young guy hadn't fallen or gone off course. He just came in last! He had a shocked, sick look on his face as he picked up his skis and approached his father, saying, "Dad, I think I'm last. That means I won't make the team. I can't believe I was that bad." His father resisted the temptation to offer platitudes such as, "You just have to get back up there," or, "All we ask is that you give it your best." Worse still would have been, "I told you we should have waxed your skis again." Instead, the dad put his hand on his son's arm and said, "I know you're disappointed, Brad. It's hard to put so much into it and not get what you expected." The son nodded, "Damn right! I thought I would at least come in third!" He leaned into his dad, who ruffled his hair and put his son's skis on his own shoulders. The impact of listening can be more profound even than words of comfort.

Listening can demonstrate love, even unconditional love. In the example of father and son, the dad's receptive listening communicated to his son how much he loved him. He was present, he listened, and in doing so gave his son the message, "You count, your feelings count. I love you equally whether you win or lose." This father didn't say a lot. He didn't have to. He listened. Expressing love is usually not identified with or even associated with listening. Most of us would expect the father to voice words of encouragement such as, "You'll do better next time." Or, we might be looking for a sort of consolation prize from the father. "Come on, I'll buy you that ski hat you've been wanting." We might even think that a loving father should give his son some timely advice. But listening is this father's gift, a gift that the son needed. Listening is a gift that all of us need. It speaks volumes.

Listening is a gift that all of us need. It speaks volumes.

We want to be able to share our doubts, our fears, our hopes, our mistakes, and our victories. In order to do so, we have to be confident that we will be heard—not judged, not blamed, not advised, and not interrupted. Sometimes, we simply need to seek release from feelings that torment us. Feelings of shame or guilt, anger or fear that are held in can fester. They can lead to depression, hopelessness, and isolation.

Kiesha is a pretty eight-year-old who was brought to us for counseling. She had been refusing to go to school, and spent most of her time alone in her room. When she arrived in our office, she appeared cautious and withdrawn. Gradually, Kiesha began to reveal her conviction that she had caused her parents' divorce. She described the arguments that she heard every night while in her room. To escape from these loud, terrifying, and heated fights, she would pray to be taken away to a magical family. When her parents did divorce, she lived temporarily with her aunt and uncle. She couldn't sleep, fearing that she might dream about the magical family and thereby cause her aunt and uncle to divorce. Through talking and being heard, Kiesha freed herself of this misplaced responsibility.

It is not only within children that unexpressed feelings can generate harmful effects. Feelings of guilt suppressed in adults can lead to low self-esteem. Feelings of shame can precipitate isolation, feelings of inferiority, and competitiveness. Such repressed feelings that are frequently distorted by obsessive reflection produce aggressive or withdrawn behavior and induce attitudes toward self and others that are destructive. A newly divorced woman had become withdrawn and depressed due to feelings of intense hurt at her daughter's rejection. Only after she described what she was enduring and let us into her sadness and crying did her depression start to lift. Then, she could respond once again to her friend's invitations.

This woman friend knew her sadness but needed to voice it. Many people don't admit threatening or unwelcome feelings even to themselves. These denied feelings could lead to bizarre and tragic behavior. The meek fellow who suddenly has a breakdown and murders his boss, the passive woman who starts to have affairs, the cautious husband and father who gambles away the family savings—these are examples of individuals at the mercy of bottled-up feelings. Finally, they exploded in destructive action. All of us knowingly or unknowingly seek a listener. We long for someone with whom we can freely describe the personal feelings that are difficult for us to accept.

Listening Gives Comfort

We especially crave a listening friend when we are suffering deep loss and sorrow. Yet it is poignantly true that these are the times when empathy is frequently absent. While doing interviews for our book *Sick and Tired of Feeling Sick and Tired: Living With Invisible Chronic Illness* (W.W. Norton, 1992), we heard this complaint repeatedly from individuals with chronic illness. "My husband doesn't want to listen," a woman would say. "My friends don't ask how I am." "My children don't seem to want to hear about my illness."

Widows and widowers often report that shortly after the funeral of a spouse, friends and family members are impatient when they hear any expressions of sorrow. Those lonely after a divorce voice a similar complaint. Their friends—even close friends—aren't willing to listen to them.

A report by a group of British researchers might provide a clue to the reason for such a lack of listening. These researchers discovered through the use of MRI (Magnetic Resonance Imaging) that when people watched their companions suffer, their brains appeared to re-create the painful experience. In effect, they really were subjectively "feeling" their loved one's pain. When people say, "I feel your pain," maybe they actually do feel that pain (*Science*, February 20, 2004, issue as reported in *The New York Times*, February 24, 2004).

Whatever the reason, however, when we need to express sorrow and seek comfort and understanding from someone else, we are often disappointed. Sharing our sorrow and being truly heard can relieve us of loneliness and provide solace. We hope that the one we speak to will truly appreciate what we are trying to say. Unfortunately, we are too often deflated and left frustrated and alone by someone who reacts to us with little understanding of our feelings.

Without the relief or the satisfaction of connection, we withdraw and resolve to keep quiet.

After the death of Paul's mother, he choked back profound feelings of loss in the press of comforting his father, arranging for the funeral, managing a thousand details of the estate, and then returning to a packed work schedule. With no time to grieve, he was stressed and became irritable. One evening after a quiet meal with two friends, he began to surrender to his sorrow. One of the friends felt such a need to comfort that she started talking about how lucky Paul was. She told him how wonderful it was that he had enjoyed such a special relationship with his mother. This friend envied Paul because she had never been close to her own mother. She told Paul that his sadness would be brief while hers had no end.

Paul nodded in apparent agreement. However, his much-needed release of feelings had been squelched. Mistaken empathy is no substitute for genuine listening. Paul's friend probably had good intentions, but she certainly had poor listening skills. She definitely provided no comfort.

Listening Provides Recognition

It's not just during times of sorrow that we need to share our feelings and needs. Most of us want to be able to share our joys as well. We hope that others will listen and connect to our good news. Unfortunately, we are often disappointed.

Janice felt a glow of pride when the hospice director invited her to become part of a small group of people who were to be trained to provide pastoral care to grieving families. She loved the volunteer work that she already did at hospice. This recognition of her competence as a caregiver thrilled her. Janice's joy was short-lived, however. When she phoned a friend to share her good news, her friend responded, "You'll be spending even more time around death and suffering families. Are you sure you want to do this? It could be very depressing!"

And later, when she told her partner about this new professional opportunity, she was asked in an exasperated tone, "How many days a week will this take?"

Our excitement at reporting the 79 we shot at our home golf course is often punctured by a buddy's retort about having several rounds in the 70s recently. Our pride in announcing our son's acceptance to a grad school is flattened by a friend's sudden soapbox speech about the "ridiculous cost of higher education." It would seem that our good news would be welcomed by all. But those whose attention we would most appreciate often ignore our joys at job promotions, successes, and victories. However, when a friend genuinely does share in our excitement or joy with real empathy, the happy news becomes even more special. And we can get much satisfaction ourselves, recognizing achievements in those we care for.

A father remarked to us,

> I love to praise my oldest son. He's only seven years old so he still has that incredible innocence. So if I say to him, "Man, you hit that ball a mile. They're still looking for it in California," he gets a smile on his face that's wild and he practically wiggles like a puppy. It's fantastic. It's as much fun for me as it is for him. He confidently listens to and believes every word I say. In contrast, I stopped telling my wife that she looks great a long time ago. She's so convinced that she's fat that she scorns any compliment.

Listening Clarifies

There are also times when our thoughts are jumbled and unfocused. We are confused as we confront bewildering events. Or we are torn between alternative ways of proceeding. We need someone to listen to us. We need help in sorting out the situation and ourselves. A young couple who had seen us for counseling wrote a note of appreciation,

> *We want you to know how much you helped us. We were at a loss and at odds with one another. We didn't know whether we should try in vitro fertilization again or whether we should try to adopt. You put us on the same page by getting us to state our thoughts and feelings. We needed to stop second-guessing one another. We're set now on adopting and we feel resolved together. Thank you so much.*

This couple had become more and more confused and indecisive in their struggle with infertility. They had been overwhelmed with advice from their family members and friends. They needed space to hear each other—space that we were able to provide by listening.

In families as well as in the business world, we face issues and decisions that can bewilder and even paralyze us. In sharing our dilemmas, we unwittingly invite opinions and suggestions that can further complicate the situation. The resulting "feedback" from others at home or at work can confuse us, and blur our own opinions. These unsolicited suggestions can even undermine our confidence to resolve our own problems. We don't need advice as much as we need a willing listener who allows us to clarify our own thoughts and make our own decisions. When someone listens, we discover the layers of our thoughts; we "peel the onion." We might even discover that our original views change dramatically.

When someone listens to us, we are given the opportunity to hear ourselves, and then to edit what we are trying to say. We have the time to qualify what we've said in order to be more exact. We can develop our thoughts free from interruption. The listener gives us the space in which we are able to say not only what we really mean, but often to know our thoughts, feelings, and opinions more clearly.

We Pay a Price for Not Listening

When we are rarely listened to, we might choose—consciously or unconsciously—to stop trying to express ourselves. The results of such a decision can be serious and damaging. A woman diagnosed with breast cancer told us:

> *I don't talk about my cancer treatments to my closest friend anymore. It was so hard. As soon as I would tell her that I felt nauseous after a treatment, she would immediately say, "You really should try the alternative treatment that Suzanne Somers is doing. I keep telling you that she's had real success without ravaging her body. We don't know the future impact on your body of all these toxins that they are putting in you." She scared the hell out of me and made me feel so unsure about what I was doing. The saddest thing is that since I can't, or won't, talk to her about chemo, I don't want to talk to her about anything. I really don't want to be with her. I'm losing my best friend just when I need every friend I can get.*

This woman's choice is similar to that made over and over by individuals who don't think they will be heard. This group includes teenagers who don't share their thoughts and actions with their parents. As a result, they lose not only the guidance and perspective that they might have received but also the closeness to their parents that sharing promotes. A spouse, fearing blame and judgment, may not admit financial and career concerns to his or her partner. As a result, however, this person sacrifices the comfort and support that sharing can provide. A woman who's sure that her boss won't listen to her will fail to offer ideas that might benefit both of them, and their employer.

Relationships at home and at work suffer when a poor listening environment chills or prevents honest expression.

Individuals keep to themselves. Loneliness ensues. Resentful presumptions develop. Distrust flourishes. As we said, loneliness can breed low self-esteem, lack of perspective, and unhealthy thoughts and actions.

It is sad when an individual develops a habit of not sharing feelings and concerns. It is sadder still when entire families suffer from a pattern or culture of non-communication. Fathers of the "old school" can be so distant that children and even spouses can be starved for words and affection. A strapping Irish businessman told us ruefully, "My dad never told me he loved me—never told any of us—but, he sure as hell told us what he didn't like. I sometimes wonder how he really was with my mom. He sure never showed her any love in public."

Similarly, some mothers are too busy and wedded to their roles as selfless servants. They don't take time to share their own feelings and needs. Teenagers can all too easily withdraw into their own private worlds. Families with problems with alcoholism or drugs often create a code of secrecy and silence. No one shares and no one listens. Habits of non-communication learned in these families can wreak havoc in their relationships. Families that fail to recognize their poor communication habits will also fail to develop or adopt more effective ones.

While the absence of real listening is debilitating to individuals and relationships, the reality of listening taking place is both liberating and productive. Listening frees us to share our doubts, our fears, our mistakes, and our victories. It can free us from the lonely hell of shame and regret, and can make our moments of happiness even more gratifying. Filled with wonder and gratitude, Sarah described the experience of being really listened to by her boss:

I made a bad mistake at work. It may cause us to lose a lot of money and probably will make our department and my boss look bad. I was so upset when I realized what I had done. I went to her right away and apologized. I told her that I was worried for her, and that I felt awful about having put her job at risk. There have been tensions between us in the past. So, I dreaded her reaction. As angry as she was, she just sat there and listened to me. She told me that she appreciated my concern for her and recognized that I was so upset. She talked about how heavy the workload has been for everyone this year and that mistakes were inevitable. I was stunned that she seemed to understand so completely where I was. She didn't give me a lecture or attack me. It was even more amazing to me because I could tell that she had to work to control her anger.

Listening at home or at work is not a luxury— it's a necessity.

The boss's response was a welcome gift for Sarah. Understanding is always far more motivating than censure.

Listening to another person can be just as rewarding as being heard. When we truly listen, we bridge the gap between ourselves and our child, partner, or friend. We learn to see things from another's point of view. We grow in understanding and become more tolerant. When we listen, we tend to judge less, have less prejudice, and edge a bit closer towards wisdom.

Listening at home or at work is not a luxury—it's a necessity.

Without it, distance grows, distrust and misunderstanding abound, and families and businesses become less cohesive, less united, less healthy, and less productive. Homes without people who are attentive and understanding are not safe settings in which to relax and to grow. Workplaces that lack listening coworkers become tense and overly competitive. "Everyone for himself and herself" is the theme. Teamwork and productivity suffer.

First, listening has to be valued. Then it has to be put into practice. A friend of ours returned from a trip to Kenya anxious to relate to us the listening ritual that she had seen practiced by members of the Masai tribe. She described the way that two tribesmen would stand very erect, facing one another. One would speak at some length. The other would say back in a rather musical tone, "uh huh, uh huh, uh huh." When the tribesman who spoke first finished, the one who had been listening started to speak. Gradually, the first speaker began to respond, "uh huh, uh huh, uh huh."

Later, our friend was amazed to see this listening ritual adopted by a British guide who had been among the Masai in Kenya for thirty years. He was speaking to another ex pat Brit in the Masai manner. One spoke while the other responded musically . . . "uh huh, uh huh, uh huh."

We can profit from rituals that demonstrate value placed on listening, especially if they also provide an opportunity to practice listening skills. For spouses and partners, the ritual might take the form of a fifteen-minute or half-hour exercise. One person shares his or her feelings or most meaningful experience for the day while the other person listens. Then, the listener shares while the former speaker listens. It might involve a daily walk or a car ride or a weekly dinner date.

In business, a manager who values the development of teamwork might take his team off-site to facilitate better communication and understanding in the staff. Or a boss might advocate and demonstrate not only an open-door policy but also an open-mind and open-ear attitude. The focus for the members of a family, the partners at the firm, the manager and his team should be on interpersonal understanding and practice in the skill of listening. When one talks the other works very hard to listen attentively before reacting. Listening clarifies while it lessens misunderstandings and slights. It provides the respectful attention which, when withheld, causes hurt, resentment, and distrust, but when given instills a sense of worth and purpose.

Reflection Questions

◎ Can you describe an occasion when you thought that someone heard you completely?

◎ Can you remember a time when you didn't listen well to someone? Do you know why you didn't?

◎ Are you aware of the ways that you react to—rather than listen to—criticism or affirmation?

CHAPTER TWO

Spouses
and
Partners

N o setting promises the comfort and safety of attentive understanding more than the home. No relationship offers the promise of joy and satisfaction from genuine empathy more than that from your spouse or partner. When your spouse or partner listens to you, you feel especially valued and even loved. Being heard affirms who we are and also validates what we are expressing. When we receive careful attention, we feel worthwhile. When we are understood, we feel less alone in our feelings and experience. In our central relationship, our need to be listened to with respect and understanding is fundamental. When this need is met, it is most satisfying. The world can be indifferent, cruel, and judgmental, but we can hope to retreat to the safety of our home and the comforting understanding of our spouse. The world might not listen,

Love is best defined as "pure attention to the being of the other."

but we need to trust that our spouse will.

Love is best defined as "pure attention to the being of the other."

In love, we attend closely to the beloved. We understand her needs and rhythms. We listen carefully to his ups and downs, ins and outs. In love, we are known more generously than we know ourselves. In that appreciative atmosphere, we can relax and grow. Caroline Richards writes in *Centering* (Wesleyan Press, 1964, p. 40):

> It is difficult to stand forth in one's growing, if one is not permitted to live through the stages of one's unripeness, clumsiness, unreadiness, as well as one's grace and aptitude. Love provides a continuous environment for the revelation of one's self, so that one can yield to life without fear and embarrassment. This is why love is in the strictest sense necessary. It must be present in order for life to happen freely. It is the other face of freedom.

Our loving central relationship should be the place where we learn to be ourselves. There at least, we should be free, safe from harsh judgment and crippling expectations. It is there that we hope to express our fears, joys, doubts, and dreams. When we are safe in this most loving relationship, we can identify with the words of the fox in Saint-Exupéry's *Little Prince* (Harcourt, Brace & World, 1943, p. 83):

> But if you touch me, it will be as if the sun came to shine in my life. I shall know the sound of a step that will be different from all the others. Other steps send me hurrying back underneath the ground. Yours will call me, like music, out of my burrow.

Couples who enjoy the safety of a trust, who listen purely and attentively to one another, know the growth-prompting power of intimacy. Every person committing himself or herself to another person does so with the hope that, with such understanding, union will be achieved. Each of us yearns to be known, affirmed by one central person whom we love. Each of us thrives when that hope is realized and when we are no longer half but whole. For us, there is no more hunger and thirst for love, no more loneliness. Children thrive in the beauty of such a parental union; friends warm themselves at the hearth of a couple with such a mutual, respectful love.

When such love is so needed and so nurturing, why is it so difficult to achieve and even more difficult to maintain? Some individuals, wanting to believe that such loving is possible, have asked us, "Do you know any happily married couples?" Most of us did not see marital bliss at home. Many of us don't see many couples content in their relationships. Statistics bear sad witness to the failure of marriages to achieve happiness. Tragically, even individuals who stay together often live lives of angry or quiet desperation. Why is "pure attention" and real listening so often replaced in the home by bickering, tension, and distance? The answer lies in the very depth of the need that we have to be known, loved, appreciated, safe, and secure at home. There are many blocks that get in the way of listening between spouses and partners. Some of the major blocks are presented below.

Blocks to Effective Listening

Block #1: Intense Emotion

When our needs are strong, so are our feelings about those needs. Strong feelings can block our efforts to listen. An acquaintance telling us that she is losing her job might engender our feelings of concern or care. A spouse reporting the same news can set off such intense emotions in us that listening becomes nearly impossible. Our needs regarding the security of our family's financial status can provoke such anxiety that listening can disappear. We might also feel frustration and suspicion that our partner may have caused the job termination or triggered the problem. Listening is the victim of intense emotion.

Powerful emotion is linked to profound need. Nowhere are our needs more pronounced than in our central relationship. In this relationship, we give our spouse or partner enormous power—the power to confirm or to deny our intelligence, our attractiveness, and our worth. The spouse becomes a mirror into which we look to see who we are. Others may see us as very special, but unless our partner does, belief in our specialness is most difficult. Others might view us as smart or talented or lovely, but if our spouse does not, we probably do not either. We grow to know ourselves in our closest relationships, and in these relationships our knowledge of ourselves can be clarified or distorted, supported or destroyed.

So, with our spouses, we can be most secure, most known, most loved. But we can also be most vulnerable. When partners share with us thoughts, feelings, and experiences, our well-being and even our sense of ourselves can be threatened. When we are under a threat, listening is not our first response. A wife might say to her husband that she is dissatisfied by the limits of their apartment. What the husband "hears" is: "You're a poor provider." A husband mentions to his wife that he would like to go on a golf trip with a few of the guys. All she hears is: "I'd have more fun with my friends than with you." When one partner fails to mention the other's new haircut or new outfit, the message heard by the other one is, "I don't find you attractive."

A thirty-year-old woman named Mary Beth complained to others about an upcoming vacation,

> *These two weeks are the only vacation time we will get this year. We both got new jobs the beginning of February, and we've been working so hard. Ray works from seven in the morning 'till three in the afternoon, and he has a forty-five minute commute. My job starts later and ends later. We barely see each other during the week. Now he wants us to spend our only vacation with his family at a reunion. I don't think he wants to do it, but he feels he's got a family obligation. What about his obligation to me? I don't understand why he isn't yearning for time just to be with me.*

Mary Beth is so filled with her own feelings of hurt and resentment that she cannot hear Ray. She is not listening to his fear of disappointing his family, or his need to see his brother and sisters, or his guilt at not having seen his mother and father for a long time. She is hearing this message about herself: "He does not want to be alone with me and doesn't care about my feelings and needs." As she hears this message about herself, she does not listen to Ray, and does not help him to sort out his feelings, needs, and commitments.

A couple, Wendy and Ron, were in their first marriage counseling session when Ron said,

> *This is our first house and it's very small. If things aren't put away, it looks gross. I wish Wendy would get into the habit of hanging up her clothes right away, or doing the dishes after dinner. It puts me on edge if things are lying around. I can't relax if things are piled up. It's how I am. So before I watch TV, I do the dishes and put stuff away. If I ask her to help out, she goes nuts. She calls me compulsive. Maybe I am a bit of a "neat freak," but I wish she'd understand that mess makes me uneasy.*

Wendy is probably not hearing Ron's discomfort, his need for order, or his hurt that she is not responding to his wishes. She is convinced that Ron is telling her that she is a slob. So, she "goes nuts." Ron fails to hear how she is seeing his behavior as criticism. He hears only that he is compulsive. Both Wendy and Ron deserve to be heard and not labeled. In listening to each other, they could also find the understanding and trust necessary to see beyond the mundane to their human need for true partnership.

Block #2: Individual Differences

Differences between spouses and partners further block their abilities to listen with patience. Opposites might attract, but they can also frustrate. Differences can be stimulating, but they can also be annoying or confusing. Ron and Wendy have different needs, habits, personalities, and pace. One of them needs order constantly; the other can live with some clutter. Complementarity demands that they share, listen with respect, and develop routines that work for both of them.

They don't have to be alike; they do have to communicate. Those personal differences have tested their relationship. The old joke about a couple coming nearly to blows because of different approaches to squeezing and capping toothpaste is more revelatory than funny. We want things done our way and can take great offense when our partners refuse to go along. "My way or the highway" captures an uncompromising and unproductive attitude toward differences. My way is right. Yours is wrong.

In their lives together, many couples are forced to navigate differences in many specific areas. These include areas such as their tastes in music, movies, literature, and home decoration as well as in more basic and pervasive ways, such as in

Personality:	introvert—extrovert
	adventurous—cautious
	laissez faire—controlling
Patterns of communication:	talkative—quiet
Expressions of physical affection:	demonstrative—reserved
Attitudes about money:	enjoy and spend—save and be secure
Religion:	Protestant, Jew, Catholic, Muslim, Atheist

Any and all of these differences between individuals attempting to live happily together can be quite positive. Differences can encourage people to grow beyond entrenched habits, to move from their complacency with the familiar. Instead, all too often, differences provoke frustration and hurt. It is easy to interpret the other person's different perspective or manner as insensitive or indifferent. A wife can read her husband's insistence on staying up after she goes to bed as a sign that he doesn't want to be close to her at the end of the day. He can see her desire for his late night companionship as a failure to understand his need for time to finish some things undone and to unwind at the end of the day. Distance and acrimony are often the result of interpreting the other's behavior as *about me*, insensitivity *toward me*, lack of care *for me*. In order for real meeting to occur, partners must hear what the other's behavior tells you about himself or herself, not what it says about you. In the example just cited, the husband must listen to his wife's needs to cuddle and be close before sleep. She has to hear his desire for precious private time before retiring. When they have truly listened to one another and have truly understood each other's needs, then they are free to act in ways that are mutually fulfilling. Maybe they will cuddle for a while before she sleeps and he gets up to enjoy private time. Or, maybe they will alternate nights when they retire together or separately. The solutions may vary, but listening without the taint of defensiveness can bring about unique benefits for both partners.

Similarly, couples frequently have different needs regarding friendships, socializing and privacy. These differences initially—and maybe always—attract individuals to one another. The extrovert, for example, can be drawn in admiration to the quiet, reflective depth of the introvert. The introvert can be energized by the social ease and confidence of the extrovert. The differences can stimulate and attract. They can also cause hurt and anger.

Linda and Kevin suffered the impact of this kind of difference. Kevin had initially felt comforted by Linda's quiet manner. He basked in her admiration of his social energy. But when his job demanded more attendance at company events and more dinners out with clients, Linda vehemently resisted accompanying him. Kevin heard her resistance as lack of support and forcefully told her so. Linda accused Kevin of selfish regard for himself and his career and of having no regard for her. Despite the hurt and disappointment, each needed to listen. Rather than simply refusing to go, Linda had to talk to Kevin about the fear and awkwardness she felt in attending company affairs. Kevin had to listen to Linda to understand how threatening these events were for the quiet, private woman he loved. Kevin had to express the awkwardness he felt at being the only executive officer at a company event without a spouse. Linda had to let go of her resentment and hear his need for her presence. Then, each could appreciate the other's needs for companionship, privacy, and understanding. Without listening, each felt hurt and each felt guilty for disappointing the one very one they loved the most. When Kevin and Linda listened, they went from low and negative feelings to feeling valued and needed. Listening has the power to communicate love, and it carries a message of worth and value.

Listening is crucial for parents who want to act as a unified team in raising their children. Frank, an angry and frustrated husband and father, described a divided and dysfunctional team in the following narrative:

> *This is a story that just never changes for us. Ever since our daughter Irene started school, Amanda has been in a pitched battle with her. I dread coming home at night after the school year starts. Irene and Amanda argue over clothes, homework, play dates, use of the phone . . . or whatever! Then Amanda turns to me, saying, "You set the rules for phone and computer time. You tell her when she has to do homework." But, when I do step in, my wife tells me that I'm not doing it right. I'm too harsh or I'm too soft. I hate it. This year I'm backing out. It's Amanda's war with Irene. I'm out of it.*

Frank and Amanda are experiencing the hurt and estrangement that differences can potentially create. They have different attitudes toward discipline and rules of behavior, and different approaches in administering them. These parents have different perceptions of the role of father and mother, and different ways of relating with their daughter. These differences have to be explored, understood, and respected. Mutual, attentive listening is the remedy for such feelings as neglect, rejection, and misunderstanding.

For example, Frank has particular needs in his relationships with his wife and with his daughter. He has strong feelings when those needs are met or not met. Similarly, his wife Amanda has her own feelings. Each must be willing to share those needs and feelings honestly and openly, and be willing to listen to the other. Frank has to state how pained he feels to see his wife and daughter constantly arguing. He has to admit his anger and hurt when Amanda puts him in the middle of these arguments, and then criticizes his performance. Amanda has to express her feelings of frustration with their daughter and her need for his support. They have to hear how much they need support from each other. Frank needs Amanda to respect his need for peace, his need for her attention which is lost in the mother-daughter battle. Frank also needs Amanda to trust him when he interacts with their daughter. Amanda yearns for Frank's comfort and understanding in her tensions with Irene. Their mutual need is obvious, but Frank's threatened "bowing out" would be a poor solution to his family's problems. In fact, that approach would only contribute further to Amanda's confusion and frustration.

Enjoying differences in others would be healthy and helpful, but many of us are more comfortable with similarity. We tend to associate with friends like us, belong to clubs and associations made up by people like us, and go to church with believers like us. Yet, we are sometimes delighted by flourishes of difference. When we visit abroad, for example, we enjoy the differences in customs, cuisine, language, architecture, and landscape. We travel to be culturally broadened by differences. We enjoy different foods and are stimulated by different tastes in music. Though we choose our partners because we are alike in central ways, we are attracted and intrigued by differences. We need to keep appreciating and enjoying these differences by listening respectfully. In so doing, we come to know our partner in all of his or her nuances and dimensions. We are thus freed from our tendency to selfishness, our proclivity to think that our way is the only way. Our partner's uniqueness is a treasure to be discovered and explored with loving attention. It is, as well, a common resource that keeps expanding our shared horizons.

> Our partner's uniqueness is a treasure to be discovered and explored with loving attention.

Block #3: Temptation to Change the Other

When we fear that our needs will not be met, our reactions thwart clear listening and trigger nonproductive behavior. We are sorely tempted to change others into people who will meet our needs. (Amanda and Frank are giving in to this temptation and are suffering the consequences.) We think, "I would be fine if only you were different—more orderly, less compulsive, more calm, more involved, more attentive, and less critical." The attempt to change someone won't be productive, especially since your spouse or partner is indulging in a similar "logic." It is a difficult temptation to combat. It would be so easy if only your spouse would change. You know your need, and you know that your partner is not meeting it. You also know so clearly how she or he could. For example, suppose you said, "I need to relax at a party and in order for that to happen, I need to be sure that my husband is not drinking too much. So I have made it clear to him—have only one beer. That's enough anyway. If he sticks to that the evening will be fine and I'll be relaxed."

No. It is not that simple. You are seeing things only through the lens of your own needs. In any relationship, both partners have needs that can be very different from and even clash with the other's. In the above example, your husband might be unhappy to be limited to one drink. Maybe he is a big guy and the evening is long. He can easily and enjoyably absorb more than one drink. Having only one beer for him is being put in a straitjacket; thus confined and anxious about your reactions, he finds little pleasure in the evening.

It might seem simple to you that to assure your relaxation at a party, you should restrict your husband's drinking. You might presume, "If he loves me, he will do that for me." Your husband, however, hears not your fear of drunkenness that stems from your childhood experiences with an alcoholic parent, but a command, "Don't drink!" He also hears your distrust of him and a judgment that he drinks too much. Finally, he hears, "You are bad and unloving if you don't follow my wishes." Hearing blame, judgment, and control, his tendency is to resent, to be angry, and to rebel. Love can't be coerced. It can't be proved by acquiescence to demands or tests. "If you love me, you won't drink." Sadly, in this dynamic each loses, each feels unloved, and each behaves in an unloving manner.

How to resolve the conundrum: if your husband drinks, you don't feel free to relax; if you command, he is not free to enjoy. Here is an effective way to solve the conundrum. Instead of telling your husband what to do or not to do, instead of focusing on *him* and trying to change *him*, you can share with him *your* needs and feelings. You can describe how fearful you feel when someone you love drinks. You can relay the tension you feel at parties and your need to relax after working hard all week at a stressful job. You can share with your husband the ghosts and memories of your childhood that haunt you. Often such self-revelation of feelings and needs exposes the speaker and makes you more vulnerable. It is easier to focus on the other and tell him what to do. "If you would drink less, I'd be fine." Easier maybe, but not productive.

If you share your feelings rather than try to control his behavior, then your husband is invited to listen to your painful self-revelation, to understand *your* needs, to be caring of *you*. He can enter *your* world of tension and need and be compassionate. He can then share his need to relax and his feelings of hurt when he hears distrust. He can admit to his tendency to rebel when told what to do. You are then called to listen to *his* feelings and to *his* needs. Then, both of you feeling respected and understood can freely act in a way that communicates the love you feel for each other.

Maybe you will become reassured and feel safe regarding his drinking alcohol. Maybe he will gladly have only one drink or beer, knowing that he is doing so freely out of love and understanding. The answer to the apparent conundrum is not an easy answer but a necessary one. It asks of you to become vulnerable, to share your own feelings, to tell him openly what is happening within you—feelings, needs, perceptions. In doing so you may feel that you risk being ignored, risk being judged. Despite your fears, though, you are opening yourself to your husband, trusting that he will listen and will want to respond to your needs. Trust invites the best of him. Telling him what to do stems from fear of the worst; i.e., he will not respond lovingly to my needs. Sadly, we tend to bring about the very thing that we fear. In focusing on him, telling him what to do, you provoke the very rejection that you fear.

In a healthy relationship between two adults, the focus of each person is on honest sharing of self and loving attention to the other. Each commits to be open, to reveal what one feels and needs, and at the same time to listen to the needs, feelings, thoughts, and opinions of the other and to respond generously and empathetically. Each is free to be devoted to the other when each is confident that the other is listening and responding in precisely the same spirit.

If we focus solely on the other's needs and ignore our own, we lose self-respect and become victims. If we focus solely on our own and expect the other to serve them, we crush the other and lose interest in him or her. The health of the relationship is in the balance between respect for self and respect for our partner. We have to be honest about our feelings and needs and trust that our partner is committed to responding freely to us. At the same time, we listen carefully to our partner, committed to being fully responsive. Establishing such mutuality of commitment is a formidable task. It is far easier and more tempting to focus solely on "what I expect from you." An antidote to this temptation to change the other is to learn to listen to what our partner feels, needs, and expects from us.

Growth in a relationship occurs when the individual recognizes, "I can only change myself, and one of the ways I need to change in this relationship is to become more understanding. I have to become a better listener." One step toward taking the focus off your own needs is to listen for the needs of your spouse. Try this revealing exercise: list the needs you believe your spouse has of you and ask your spouse to do the same. Then compare lists.

One couple we were counseling was shocked at their reactions to the lists. Jennifer realized that in each of Jay's needs that she listed—a warm welcome when he arrives home, more frequent sex, help with his community board meetings—she heard criticisms of her. At the same time, she felt irritated and critical of him for having these needs. She knew his needs but did not accept them. Jay, on the other hand, had to admit that he had not really reflected on what Jennifer needed from him. He had been too focused on what he needed from her. Jennifer could only respond to Jay's needs when she heard them not as criticism. She truly heard these needs when she listened more deeply to Jay, and heard *about him* rather than *about her*. Jay realized that he also was suffering from self-focus at the cost of not listening to and not knowing Jennifer's needs. The sound of our own needs can drive us inward, away from the one we most love.

Knowing your spouse's needs, affirming those needs as lovingly as possible, and then responding to them is an essential part of genuine meeting. That does not mean that you should ignore your own needs. You must be aware of them and you must communicate your needs clearly to your spouse. In this way, you give your partner the opportunity, as well as the challenge, to listen to you.

Block #4: No Time

A frequent complaint we hear from couples regarding their communication is "We don't have time." It takes time to speak about feelings, experiences, and reflections, and it takes time to listen attentively. Angela and Jack voiced the familiar sentiment. They had three children in their first four years of marriage. As Jack said, "That set the pace for the rest of our lives. We never have time. We've been married six years, and I don't think we've been alone for a whole weekend during the entire six years." Angela added that even before the children were born, Jack's mother had lived with them because his father had died six months before their wedding. Both believed that they were good parents, but as a couple they were not as close as they once had been. Consequently, sex had become very infrequent.

Events, children, work schedules—all can war against intimacy. Pressures that inhibit intimacy are ever-present. A corporate culture that values hard work and commitment as measured in time at the office, willingness to travel, and openness to move anywhere the company dictates is not friendly to, and can even be antithetical to, family values of closeness. Children's activities such as sports, scouts, dance lessons, and play dates can leave little time for intimacy between a mom and dad. Even community and church involvement can make time together for spouses scarce. These external pressures are insistent. They are pressing demands in the moment and they require immediate attention. Intimate time together is put off, either consciously regarded as less important, or simply forgotten.

Then there are pressures that reveal personal priorities. When Rachel complained in counseling that she never has time to talk with her boyfriend, she explained that both had part-time jobs on top of their full-time employment. They needed the extra work because they had rented a two-bedroom apartment and each had an expensive new car. Their choice for more space and flashy cars required more income. It also meant that they saw less of each other. When a couple states, "We have no time," it usually means that they have made listening and the intimacy it produces a lesser value to other priorities.

Spending time together, however, is not a luxury; it is a major priority. The children will suffer, even work will suffer, if distance in your central relationship replaces closeness, while loneliness turns into bitterness. Children are secure with parents who are united. Partners are productive when they are happy. So it is imperative that couples make it a priority to spend time alone together. Angela and Jack made necessary changes. They established Wednesday as a "date night," and they remain faithful to it. As Angela put it, "It's great. We get out of the house, have dinner together. Sometimes we go to a movie. I just want to be with him like I did when we first dated." Beyond their weekly date, Angela and Jack have begun the communication ritual that we mentioned in Chapter One. They set aside one half-hour a day, usually at the same time each day and in the same place, during which each one talks in turn about whatever feelings and thoughts have occurred that day. The listener is clearly designated. Then the listener becomes the speaker and relates thoughts and feelings, while the other listens. Angela and Jack, like so many couples who do this exercise, attested to its beneficial effects. Jack said, "I can't believe how much closer we have become. I know her more now than I did the last seven years." The exercise, like the weekly date, is a ritual that affirms the value of taking time to develop and to celebrate intimate connection.

Block #5: Reverting to Pre-Marriage Roles

Husbands and wives face a unique challenge in understanding one another. The person whom they thought they knew before marriage can appear to be quite a different individual afterward. A fellow named Darren described being "blindsided" one year into his marriage with Martina. They had met in Chicago when both worked in the financial district. Life with Martina in Chicago, Darren said, was fast-paced and exciting. After the wedding, they moved back to Martina's hometown in Connecticut. Darren found a new job on Wall Street in New York. "Overnight," Darren claims, "my wife turned into somebody else. She doesn't want to drive on I-95, she's afraid to look for a job in New York and talks more to her mom than to me. It's like she reverted to being Mommy's little girl instead of the sharp, exciting woman who had a high-paying job in Chicago."

Many young spouses feel Darren's bewilderment. The persons they fell in love with can change significantly when becoming a wife or husband. In creating their own family, spouses can readily revert to the role that they played in their original family. The person who was quiet and passive—the good girl—at home might break out to be daring and bold during and after college and later slide into her old behavior patterns when she is back "in the family." Again, the guy who was fun and social in young adulthood, when married, might become the serious planner he had been as the "sensible" oldest child.

Marty, for example, was very affectionate while dating Annie when they were newly out of law school. After their marriage, he gradually became aloof, just as he had been while growing up in a family with a dominating mother. The "avoidance of mom" behavior he had learned as a child returned as he unconsciously distanced himself from Annie, the new central woman in his life. Similarly, Sheila was self-confident and assertive in college. After having three children, she reverted to playing the role of the self-effacing peacemaker, a role she'd learned at home. Habits and roles that were formed during years of growing up may not be evident when living away from the family. But they can reappear in a new family setting.

Couples affected by feelings of confusion and even distress at witnessing changes in their partners need to share these feelings without judgment and blame. Withdrawing in disillusionment or attacking with blame ("What is wrong with you? Was that all an act in college before we got married?") does not lead to a re-connection or understanding. Feelings and needs have to be shared, and listening has to be practiced to sort out the changes that they are both experiencing. In the above example, Darren has to identify feelings of hurt at Martina's growing dependence on her mother and his need to be her confidant as he was earlier. He needs to admit his disappointment at her fear and caution, and his need for the exciting companion he delighted in before their move back East. Martina, to connect with Darren, will have to fight off defensiveness and listen to his feelings and his need for her. While these interactions will not be easy, they are absolutely necessary for growth in trust and intimacy. The person Martina was in Chicago is probably the true Martina. Away from home, she was free to be herself. Now, she needs Darren's support and understanding to break old habitual ways of acting, old expectations that she and others have of her. With his understanding, she can become the person that both she and Darren desire.

In our central relationships, our partners have the potential to fulfill our needs, to nurture our growth, to call us to be whole, happy, and peaceful. In this kind of relationship, you can love, cherish, and understand another person in many ways that never grow stale or tired. With this person, you can safely learn how to appreciate and value yourself even as you are challenged constantly to grow. The goal is worth every effort, but the effort is not easy. As Rilke said in his *Letters to a Young Poet*,

> For one human being to love another: that is perhaps the most difficult of all our tasks . . . the work for which all other work is but preparation. Love . . . is a high inducement to the individual to ripen, to become whole, to become whole for himself for another's sake: it is a great, exacting claim upon him, something that calls him to vast things. . . .

Learning to listen deeply to the one you love while listening honestly to your own feelings and needs, and being free to share them, is the path to the goal of profound intimacy as well as the means to that end.

Reflection Questions

. . . .

◉ What emotions block you in listening to your spouse or partner – fear, anger, hurt, impatience, affection, love?

◉ Can you state the needs you have of your partner or spouse?

◉ Are you confident that you have heard the needs that your partner or spouse has expressed to you?

CHAPTER THREE

Parents
and
Children

There is a reason some adults choose not to be parents. The responsibility of parenting is immense. We have the awesome task of raising a totally dependent child to be healthy in mind, body, and spirit. Our children look to us to establish who they are, to see that they are lovable, attractive, intelligent, and worthwhile. If we take the time to talk to them, play with them, be with them, then they internalize a sense of worth. They learn that they matter. If we are present at their activities, interested in their thoughts, attentive to their needs, then they can sense that they are interesting and worthwhile. If we delight in them, they can grow to feel delightful. If we hug them, listen to them deeply, and understand and appreciate their particular way of being; if we tell them consistently and in a thousand ways how much we love them, then they can learn to believe, no matter what any mean "friend" or impatient teacher says, that they are lovable.

Sensible adults know that being a parent carries this sacred responsibility. No relationship is more powerful. The child is dependent on the parent's response, vulnerable to the parent's word, attitude, and behavior. The French essayist Montaigne captured the challenge,

> To storm a breach, conduct an embassy, govern a people, these are brilliant actions; to scold, laugh and deal gently and justly with one's family and oneself . . . that is something more rare, more difficult, and less noticed in the world.

Though as parents we might at times feel helpless, to our children we can appear all-powerful. A cross word, a raised eyebrow, let alone sarcasm or scathing criticism, can destroy self-esteem. It is so much easier to tear down than to build up.

Making the relationship especially challenging is that as parents we have a dual function:

One—to give the loving trust that allows the child to explore, make decisions, and become increasingly independent.

Two—to provide the boundaries, directions, safety, lessons, values, and beliefs without which the child would lack the tools necessary to become self-reliant.

Relating with your child requires a delicate balance between these two responsibilities. First and foremost, you have to love with careful attention. This loving attention guides the second responsibility, which is to know when and how to step in with boundaries and lessons. Sometimes the choice is clear. Alert and attentive, the mother sees the toddler wobbling toward the basement stairs and swoops him to safety. No debate there. The mother acts instinctively. Sometimes the choice is not at all evident. For example, a mother learns that her fourteen-year-old daughter wants to have a flower tattooed on her ankle. She has listened to the reasons that range from "It's cool" to "All the kids are getting them." Does she demonstrate trust for her daughter and say, "Yes"? Or does she hear that her daughter is simply capitulating to peer pressure and say, "No." The right choice of the toddler's mother is evident; the teen's mother's is not. Yet each must be guided by attention and love, and each must listen deeply to what the child really needs. It is safety over delight in exploring for the toddler, and perhaps freedom from peer pressure over self-expression for the teen.

This attentive listening establishes a profound connection with the child; a level of understanding and trust develops that makes the delicate balance less in danger of tipping into domination, rebellion, permissiveness. A bright, tall seventeen-year-old boy described trust in his parents,

My mom is on my case a lot. She worries. Sometimes she bugs me. My dad is more rational. But I know that they both love me. They want what's best for me. When I'm calm, I can even tease my mom about worrying. Overall, I think we do pretty well. I'll miss them like mad when I leave for college.

He then went silent and teared up.

Tracy, an articulate, petite fourteen-year-old told us of her growing closeness to her mother,

My mom and I fought like anything when I was in junior high school. She was against my friends, the way I dressed. She was always on me about my room. I hated being at home. I can't believe the change since we came for counseling. My mom really listens now. I tell her stuff I never would have. And, I've changed, I know. It's not easy for her being a single mom. I help her out a lot now. We can even shop together now. It's awesome!

The parent has to listen at each stage of the child's development, at each unfolding without stepping too heavily in a way that could squelch unique growth, without being too close in a way that could crowd independence or too far away in a way that could terrify or allow harm. Focused, loving attention to the changing needs of the child will guide the parents' actions: one moment providing space for exploration, another providing boundaries for safety. Attentive listening facilitates creation of this balance that ultimately produces a bond between parent and child that comforts, guides, challenges, and frees.

The parent-child relationship can provide exquisite pleasure in a mutual meeting of needs. The child's need for the warmth and safety of a father's embrace is met by the father's delight in the child's trust. A mother's joy in her child's happiness and success is echoed in the child's basking in her attention. The child's need for Dad to throw the ball to her, to carry her when she is tired, to read to her before she sleeps is life-giving to a loving father. The devoted parent knows the deeply satisfying meaning of supplying nourishment not only to growing bodies but to growing minds, and developing emotions.

But as Montaigne writes and the Beatles sing, "You know it ain't easy." As much joy as the parent-child relationship can bring, it demands daily effort, discipline, and commitment. It requires skill, particularly the skill of excellent communication. There are inherent blocks to making real empathic connections, to making this relationship work, and when it doesn't, it is disappointing, frustrating, and even heartbreaking. Recognition of these blocks to effective listening paves the way to a mutually satisfying relationship with your child. There are classic listening blocks between parents and children.

Blocks to Effective Listening

Block #1: Children's Developing Stages

The parent has to learn and relearn how to listen to the child as he or she progresses from an utterly helpless baby who is thoroughly dependent to a child, teenager, and young adult who is constantly pursuing independence. A beleaguered mother told us, "I loved it when she was a baby. I always felt as if I knew what she wanted. I could tell a tired cry from a hungry cry and lot of cries in between. Now she's three, and I'm clueless. She fights me about everything. I honestly don't understand her." The once confident mother feels defeated.

Other parents describe their difficulty in listening to their teenaged children. A concerned couple voiced the complaint of countless parents of teenaged boys, "He won't talk. We ask him about school. He says, 'Fine.' He doesn't talk about his friends or about anything else. This is a kid who told us everything just last year." Failing to "listen" to his distance as natural stage for a boy in his early teens, these parents had begun to pursue their son with questions, "How's your friend Tommy doing?" "What are your teachers like?" "Why do you stay in your room?" Their questions, like most questions, hide the questioner's feelings and thoughts while asking their son to reveal his. This kind of interrogating conversation does not elicit much sharing. These parents are hearing their son's silence as signs of a problem, unhappiness, or even of hostility toward them. He is probably hearing their questions as annoying intrusions or as irrelevant inquiries. The more frustrated they get, the more he will hear what they say as criticism and blame, "You act like you are not part of this family." "What do you do in your room all the time?" He is not hearing their confusion, concern, or hurt. He is hearing that he is wrong or bad. Tension and misunderstanding easily replace harmony.

The parents could have been patient and heard their son's silence as a normal desire for privacy, and as an adolescent's predictable search for independence. They would not have been hurt or frustrated. They would not have felt the need to pursue him with endless, fruitless questions. This boy's parents could have found ways to express their interest and attention in a non-blaming, non-badgering fashion. "We miss you. Come watch the movie with us." "Classes must be demanding by the look of the books you're bringing home." The son needs to know that his parents are there for him, and that they care. He will be revealing more later.

At that time, the parents should be prepared to listen, withholding their questions and advice. Nothing elicits sharing more than the give and take of listening. When parents and children learn to listen to one another, respect and understanding of one another's needs soon develops. Relationships can then provide deep satisfaction in meeting needs, rather than in clashing over them.

As children grow, so do rivalries and clashes between brothers and sisters. This often presents another summons for the parents to listen. How different sibling rivalry would be if parents would listen rather than become judge and jury. Each child deserves to be free to tell a parent what he or she is feeling. Feelings. That's what the parent must listen for, not for accusations against a brother or a sister, and not for commands to "make him stop." The parent's job is to listen to each child, and then—if necessary—help the children to resolve the issue. The temptation is to get a quick fix that blames one child. But this approach will always backfire. What child will want to talk to a parent or trust a parent's love if he or she feels that the parent favors his or her sibling?

An added temptation for parents is to saddle children with a judgment. A woman in her forties spoke about her childhood with strong emotion, "I hated being told I was too sensitive. Any time I tried to talk about my feelings—like being hurt by a friend or being embarrassed about something—I'd hear, 'You're too sensitive.'" Parents can unwittingly judge rather than listen: "You are selfish!" "You're just shy." "You're so bossy." "You're sweet." These labels, coming from all-powerful parents, can land on vulnerable, developing children with crushing force. A parent tired of a child's complaints or frustrated with a child's demands can too easily forgo listening to the child and resort to name-calling.

Different ages and stages of a child's development can arouse particular emotions for the parent that are really rooted in his own childhood. These emotions can block calm listening. A father of a young boy told us of an insight into himself that he had recently gained.

When I was little, my mom was in the army, and we moved three times before I was in fifth grade. I was constantly by myself and had a hard time making friends. So, when my son, a third-grader, came home from school complaining that he had no friends, I tightened up and started loading him down with advice. I was dying to keep him from suffering the loneliness that I went through. But he said, "No, Dad, it's OK. I've got a plan. I'm sitting on the bus with Duncan. Shawn will be in Little League with me and Damon does karate. So, soon I'll be OK." I was amazed. He's not going through what I did. I was putting my stuff on him.

The dad's fears were keeping him from listening; instead he was projecting his own childhood onto his son. A daughter's weight gain can trigger a similar panic and block to listening in a mother who felt fat in childhood. A parent who struggled in school may push a child too hard who has similar academic difficulties. Relationships that had been close and marked by easy connection and understanding can suddenly become tense and confrontational at another stage of development.

Block #2: Responsibility of Parenting

Parents have the responsibility to impart certain moral and social values to their children. They also have the job of instilling religious beliefs and communicating family and ethnic traditions. In addition, moms and dads are expected to provide security, education, and opportunities for pleasure, exploration, self-expression, and growth. A parent's pursuit of this formative agenda can make listening to the child problematic.

Suppose your teenager decides that he no longer wants to attend Temple with the family. If you and your spouse see it as your duty to inculcate religious beliefs and practices, you might not want to hear your son explain why he's reluctant to attend the service. You tend to hear his complaint as a rejection of your faith. When should you insist that your son practice a certain behavior? When should you cease and desist the effort? The wise answer is not an easy one. But it will not emerge from poor listening. Your teenager may not be rejecting the faith that is so dear to his parents. If you hear such a rejection and enforce his attendance, your decision may be based on a false premise. If you hear that you've failed as parents, you will suffer feelings of guilt or anger unnecessarily. As parents, you must arrive at a sound decision about attending religious services. Listen carefully as your teenager explains his reluctance. As parents, you should listen to the meaning your child places on attendance. How does he or she connect the practice of attending a service to faith? This kind of listening can be very revealing to you and your child. It can lead not only to greater connection and understanding but also to a decision that provides family peace rather than anger and hurt.

Parents have to know and live the values, morals, and beliefs that they are attempting to impart. They should also understand the meaning behind the rules they establish. A successful lawyer explained his antipathy toward the religion in which he was raised: "We'd get to Mass late and leave after communion. It was a joke. There wasn't any sense of prayer or belief. We were punching a clock. Then, the church made you feel that you were bad. It was the same message I always got from my dad. It was all hypocrisy."

The lawyer heard no message of love from his church. Nor did he experience any sense of the sacred while attending mass. If going to Mass was a profound, spiritual event for his parents, they did not share that attitude with him. If loving others was a foundational message for one's life, this man's father didn't pass it on. Children absorb the values their parents model, and there are no shortcuts in values education. "Do what I say not what I do" is a doomed message. Despite signs to the contrary, children really are always watching their parents. Consciously or unconsciously, they take many of their cues from the values and cherished beliefs of their moms and dads.

As parents, we fulfill our mission to impart values by living them. But we do not teach only by example. We are forced in one situation after another to decide how to instruct our children. Do we insist on obedience to a rule, or do we choose to make an exception? Do we step forward to decide a course of action for our children, or do we let go and permit a child to make a decision and learn from it? For example, your child might say, "I don't want to go to Grandma's house. It's boring." You have to ask yourself, "Is this a time to insist on obedience, or should I allow my child to decide?" The choice is more likely to be harmonious for the parent and child if they listen to each other. Is the child really bored, or is he embarrassed? Does he really want to play with his friends, or is he currently tired from an overload of family activities? Do you want your child to go because you don't want Grandma's feelings to be hurt? Is refusing to allow your child to stay home a question of safety? Is it a question of setting a precedent for other siblings? If we don't know the answers to these questions, we can't make thoughtful decisions. You must first listen to yourself and then to your child.

Block #3: Seeing Children as a Reflection of Yourself

If you view your child's experience as a measure of your own competence, you will hinder your ability to empathize with your child's unique experience. This failure to listen is unfair to your child who deserves your undivided attention. It is also unfair to you. Your child's experience of failure or crisis is painful enough for you, without taking on responsibility for it. Many parents are quick to take such responsibility if a son or daughter is unsuccessful. They do not claim credit if the child succeeds—only blame if he or she should fail.

In addition, this tendency to see our lives reflected in our children's lives leaves us vulnerable and open to self-doubt. How can adults be effective parents if they are overly sensitive and reactive to any message they might hear as critical? This orientation makes it harder for parents to really listen objectively to their children.

Example #1

> **The child says**: "I would be so happy if I weren't so fat."
>
> **The parent hears**: "You gave me bad genes." "You didn't provide a proper diet for me."
>
> **The child is really saying**: "I'm vulnerable." "I'm afraid that the other girls are prettier."

Example #2

> **The child says**: "We don't go on neat vacations like my friend's family does."
>
> **The parent hears**: "You're cheap." "We're poor."
>
> **The child is really saying**: "I feel awkward when other kids talk about their vacations. I'm afraid they think I'm not cool."

Being a responsible parent and having some confidence at being successful is challenging and hard earned. With so many challenging concerns—sexuality, religion, drugs, education, etc.—even the most competent individuals can be plagued by self-doubt. A safe and sure path to greater satisfaction is to listen, particularly when your child is talking about issues that involve your role as teacher and guardian.

While many parents are vulnerable to doubts about their effectiveness, they may also be very sensitive about what others think of them. We might not admit it, but we may be tempted to bolster or protect our own egos with our children. After all, if your children are reflections of you, their triumphs or failures also belong to you. Sporting a Yale decal on the rear window of their SUV, many parents are making an announcement to the world about themselves. The Yalie daughter probably doesn't even have a Yale decal on her own car. We take pride in our children's sports and academic achievements. We boast about their successes and bask in the reflected glory. Unless we are very honest and very careful, our need for them to achieve can be propelled by our own need to look good. This could definitely blind us to the needs our children have to be seen clearly.

Parents attending parent/teacher meetings are likely to hear statements about their own children as reflections of their parental success or deficiencies. "Your child is doing marvelously and gets along beautifully with the other children." That statement may be heard as: "What a wonderful job you have done in raising this child." Conversely, a statement complaining that "your son is not working up to capacity and shows signs of aggression and a tendency to bully," could seem like a serious indictment of the boy's mother or father. Because we have difficulty in separating our egos from the misfortunes or achievements of our children, we find it hard to hear messages that are just about them.

The same pride or shame by association can distort the messages we receive from our children. When our child expresses admiration for a friend's father, we are tempted to reply, "Are you telling me I'm not as good a dad?" When our child says, "I really like the game Grandpa gave me," we quickly retort, "Did you write him a thank-you card?" Maybe the reminder comes from a desire to teach our children manners. But this parent might also be prompted by the fear that Grandpa will be judging her parental performance. A child might proudly tell her mother, "I told my teacher that I babysat my sister last night." The mom may agonize that the teacher might have gotten the wrong impression of her. "Did you tell her that I had to work and that I wasn't out partying?" the mother responds. Her reaction fails to listen to the child's pride in babysitting.

Our own ego needs may also block us from providing the loving, freeing attention that our children need. A talented but tense young man told us how hard it would be to tell his parents that he was dropping out of medical school to become a teacher. "It will be very hard for them to accept or to understand. They want to be able to go to the club and say, 'My son, the doctor . . .'" A sixteen-year-old related a similar pressure from his dad: "I don't want to go out for football next season. I just don't want to play. I don't like the coach and I'd rather have the time to get my grades up, and then play basketball. But I hate the thought of telling my dad. He loves going to games and thinks I'll make all-conference." The medical school student and the sixteen-year-old—in fact, all of our children—should be able to trust that their parents will relate to them agenda-free. They need our self-less support to sort out their priorities, values, and feelings. When they trust that we are there for them, they can listen to our views, opinions, and suggestions. Listening to them freely and deeply must precede any advice we might offer. The loving focus needs to be on them, not on us!

The loving focus needs to be on them, not on us!

Block #4: Conflicting Needs of Child and Parent

Parents and children often have difficulties hearing one another when their needs are in apparent conflict:

- The parent's need to assure the child's safety *vs.* the child's need to explore

- The parent's need to teach the child to work *vs.* the child's need to play

♦ The parent's need to control *vs.* the child's need to be
   independent

It is the nature of the child to evolve from dependence to
independence. It is the mission of the parent to protect,
guide, teach, and nourish. The separate agendas of parents
and their offspring can make listening to one another a
threatening exercise. If a ten-year-old boy listens to his
parents' concern for his asthma, his desire to play soccer
might be threatened. If a mom or dad hears and
sympathizes with their thirteen-year-old daughter who
wants to sleep overnight at a friend's house where no adult
will be present, then that parent's need to protect a child
might be compromised. A child frequently has wants. He or
she wants material things, wants to stretch boundaries,
wants permission for this and that. As Bill Cosby as
Heathcliff Huxtable in *The Cosby Show* complains, "Why
does a child start every sentence with 'Dad can I. . . ?" At
these times, the child doesn't want to listen and doesn't even
want to be heard. He or she wants only a "Yes," "OK, " or
"Go ahead." Parents want their children to be safe, polite,
busy with chores and homework. They do not want to listen
to endless requests. It's not easy for children or parents to
listen to each other when the "Can I have . . ." or "Can I
do . . ." requests begin. The following exchange highlights
the conflicting needs of a mother and son—and their lack of
good listening skills.

Mom: There is no way on earth that you can take the car for
the weekend.

Son: Carter's father always lets him take the car.

Mom: Then ask Carter's father.

Son: He's away this weekend. Everyone is going.
Everybody says my parents are too strict.

Mom: I'm not too strict. I'm sensible. Have you thought about what it would be like to live with another family?

Son: Many times!

Neither the mother nor her son slows down to attend to the other's needs or feelings. Mom might be frustrated with a request that she can't fulfill. She might be fearful about letting her son drive late at night. There may also be anxieties about her son caving in to group pressure, and then driving too fast or driving after drinking. Probably, the son is embarrassed that his friend Carter has a car available when he doesn't. The young man fears that his friends will say that his parents treat him like a child. He is resentful and doesn't feel trusted.

This mother and son still have time to listen to one another, show respect, offer understanding, and come to a compromise. It would take great effort, but it would still be rewarding. But these scenarios too frequently unfold leaving people with only frustration and pain.

Down deep, children know and understand that their parents won't always agree with them. They know that parents will sometimes feel the need to say "No." The more that children experience respect and trust which is communicated through honest listening, the more they will eventually honor their parents' values and wishes. Despite their fears for the welfare of their children, parents want their children to become independent and self-reliant. Parents and children have to learn to express understanding of the other's needs and feelings. The wise parent, listening deeply to a child's real needs for self-confidence, self-respect, success, and self-affirmation, learns to meet those needs by demonstrating trust, respect, and delight. Then the child can grow toward the very independence he or she seeks. Despite immediate clashes of interest, sensible parents and their growing children really have the same long-term goals.

Relationships between parents and their children that are marked by loving attention and careful listening create a family atmosphere that fosters growth. It is also a social climate featuring few tensions but many incidents of sharing and good humor. When family members trust that they are understood and valued, mutual teasing can be innocent and lighthearted. Laughter erupts frequently. A feeling of loving support is ever-present. The goal of all of this is so inviting, so attractive. The means to this goal is the skill of attentive listening—a working description of loving.

Reflection Questions

@ Can you list the needs that your mother and father have or had for you?

@ When is it particularly difficult to listen to your child or children?

@ Can you identify occasions when you really heard your child and communicated that understanding? Has that occured with your parent?

CHAPTER FOUR

Professionals
and
Clients

Some human relationships are challenging because the goals of the people involved are inherently at odds. There's the child wanting independence who challenges the parent concerned for the child's safety. There's the introverted spouse who wants privacy trying to cope with the extroverted partner who desires a wider social life.

The professional-client relationship would seem to be simpler and less complicated. The client/patient needs a specific service provided by an expert—a lawyer, priest, doctor, therapist, accountant, social worker. The client chooses the particular professional to attend to this need. The professional has the expertise to provide this service. In an ideal situation the client/patient presents his or her problem. The professional listens and then provides the necessary information. The client leaves the meeting satisfied, the expert, fulfilled. Sadly, however, such satisfying interactions don't take place very frequently. As Shakespeare would say, "'Tis a consummation devoutly to be wished" (*Hamlet* III, i, 55).

We do wish for this satisfaction. We need it. In the confusing complexity of life, we often lack the information we need to function responsibly. At these times, we can turn to the appropriate professional to guide us through the rocky shoals of ignorance or indecision. Without the professional's knowledge in tax matters, health issues, or legal disputes, we would be terrified and lost because we lack the expertise. Finding the professional counselor or therapist who will listen to our doubts, confusions, and questions and then direct us with clarity is a tremendous relief. Trust in such a person can dissolve anxiety and enable us to reach our goals.

Anatole Broyard, the former editor of *The New York Times Book Review*, who was dying of cancer, wrote about what he hoped his doctor could provide:

> My ideal doctor would be my Virgil, leading me through my purgatory or inferno, pointing out the sights as we go. He would resemble Oliver Sachs, the neurologist who wrote *Awakenings* and *The Man Who Mistook His Wife for a Hat*. I can imagine Dr. Sachs entering my condition, looking around at it from the inside like a benevolent landlord with a tenant, trying to see how he could make the premises more livable for me (from an article in *The New York Times Magazine* titled "Doctor, Talk to Me").

Broyard's ideal doctor embodies qualities essential for a successful professional meeting with the client.

The professional is knowledgeable. The professional can only guide safely if he or she knows the way and is thoroughly informed. The accountant who's not up to speed on all tax code changes and ramifications can't advise wisely. The physician who is winging it and isn't aware of research findings, new medications and all of their side-effects might actually steer his patient into harm's way. The diplomas and certificates on the wall announce the professional's education and training. They imply competence. The professional's responsibility is to ensure that the certificates and diplomas reflect the truth.

The professional listens. Broyard describes the ideal professional as "entering" the patient's condition, knowing it "from the inside." If the professional is not knowledgeable, he or she has no right to hang up a shingle. If this person does not listen well, being an effective professional is impossible. The professional cannot guide if she does not understand the client's particular concerns, goals, and questions. She cannot connect with the client unless she listens to his feelings. Only by listening will the professional win the client's trust. It is this trust that allows the client to listen and follow the professional's directions.

Broyard shared his image of the ideal doctor. Several doctors we know gave us their profile of the ideal patient.

Two characteristics were present in all of their depictions. First of all, the patient was clear in articulating personal needs and difficulties. Second, the ideal patient listened carefully. If the patient wants to be understood by the doctor, she stands a much better chance if she is clear and gets to the point. What are the symptoms, concerns, or questions? When and specifically how are they experienced? If the client/patient is to gain from the interaction with this professional, she or he has to listen to the expert's questions, warnings, and suggestions. An unprepared client is as irresponsible as an uninformed professional. A client who fails to listen undermines the value of the expert-client meeting as surely as the professional with the same failing.

We require professional service. Experts abound to provide it. When we receive it, life can be so much less stressful. We know that our taxes will be done. We are reassured about our blood pressure. We feel relieved, understood, respected. Life seems a bit or a lot easier. Yet, professional-client relationships that could be satisfying are often terribly disappointing. Broyard was writing about the ideal doctor because he found real ones so lacking. Patients complain that their doctors don't listen. Teachers despair that their students will ever pay attention to them. Clients can't get their lawyers to focus on what they are trying to say. Professionals sense that they're wasting their time with non-listening or inattentive clients.

What makes accurate, attentive listening so difficult between professionals and their clients? There are many typical blocks to effective listening between professionals and their clients or patients.

Blocks to Effective Listening

Block #1: Vulnerability

Listening clearly and calmly is not easy when we fear what will be said about us. What patient has not sat in a doctor's waiting room fearing bad news? Is the lump cancerous? Is my cholesterol dangerously high? Will I need surgery? What client hasn't anticipated word from the lawyer that he will have to go to court, or that the case will cost a fortune? What students haven't dreaded what the teacher would say about their essays? As clients, we are vulnerable to feeling stupid, wrong, bad, or sick. When we are afraid, we tend not to listen well. Imagine these parents listening to their lawyer as she advises them about their son's upcoming court appearance.

> *You will have to be at court about an hour before we are scheduled to go in. I don't know when we will be called, but you have to be prepared. James has to wear a suit and tie, and get*

rid of his attitude. This judge is tough on kids who are accused of driving irresponsibly, and tends to be particularly hard on first-time offenders. I told you that we have a good case. But, there is the possibility that the parents of the other kids in the car will cooperate with the police to place more blame on James. That may minimize their culpability. Of course, we might not have that problem because they don't have much room to bargain.

How well do you think the parents listened? Overwhelmed with fear about their son's future, they might not have heard anything more than that the "judge is tough." What time they should be in court, how their son should dress, how he should act, and what was said about the other boys—all could be lost in their fear. The stakes are high for these parents. Their vulnerability and that of their son could well impair their ability to listen well to their lawyer, and later to the judge.

Not only do we not listen well when we are vulnerable, we also usually have difficulty expressing ourselves. Consequently, we aren't heard. A psychiatrist told us about a man who was describing his father's condition, the apparent onset of Alzheimer's disease.

When I asked him how long his father had been forgetting, he said he couldn't remember. We both laughed at that, but the rest of what he said didn't help very much in determining a diagnosis. He started telling me about his father's military career as a pilot in the Air Force. That was back in the Korean War. Then he told me that the father earned a Purple Heart. He went on to describe what his father was like as a disciplinarian. I realized that this son needed to tell me that his father was a special man. He wanted to contrast what his father had been with the old man presently in this sad condition. But, time was flying by, and I still didn't have the details of the recent crisis.

Clearly this man was scared about his father's condition. In his vulnerability, he dreaded the changes taking place in his father. He was loquacious at a time when the professional needed him to be succinct. She needed short, clear descriptions of the symptoms so that she could make an accurate diagnosis and plan treatment for her patient. A minister described a similar kind of dilemma that often arises in the planning of funerals.

People often want to tell me about their loved ones. I dearly want to listen to everything they want to tell me. But in their grief, they can get so wrapped up in telling me stories about the person who died or about their own fears of the future, they often neglect to focus on details for the funeral. I have to bring them back to a discussion of the funeral itself, but it's tough. Their need to talk about their loved one actually gets in the way of making decisions for the funeral. They desperately want a funeral that personally honors this family member, but they are too overwhelmed with grief to address the task.

The client is often aware of her own vulnerability; she would probably be surprised to learn that the professional can be hampered by similar feelings. While the expert is trying to listen, to understand the client, to attend to the nuances of the case, he can be affected and distracted by fears:

◆ Am I going to be able to help this client?

◆ Do I understand what she is getting at?

◆ Does the client like me, or is she impatient?

◆ Will she be angry at what I have to tell her?

◆ Is she comparing me to her last doctor?

◆ Will she refuse to pay if she's dissatisfied?

◆ Am I measuring up to what she heard about me?

♦ How do I look? How do I sound? How am I coming across?

Professionals can look confident and secure in their well-appointed offices. As humans, however, they can feel all the insecurities that their clients feel. An elegant doctor with years of experience shared his frustration with himself:

> *I hate to admit that after so many years of practice, I still find it difficult to tell someone that his or her illness is terminal. Sometimes I hear things come out of my mouth that make me cringe. I'm not referring to bad language or inaccurate information. I mean when I see someone terrified of the news that I'm giving them, I want so badly to make them feel better that I'll fudge on the seriousness of the patient's condition. So I'll say, "Research is coming up with new treatments all the time." or "You have to be optimistic." These are not particularly bad things to say. Some might even say they are good thoughts, but I know I'm only saying them, because I don't like being the bearer of bad news, not because I believe in them.*

Clients don't see the vulnerabilities of professionals. To the client, they appear articulate and secure. At least, they don't seem to be insecure. They are in their "uniforms"—a white jacket, Roman collar, or business suit. They are on their turf: a doctor's office, rectory, university campus, or business office. Clients can see the trappings of power, professionalism, and achievement and feel woefully inferior. The professional might misread the insecurity in a client who seems angry, aggressive, cold, distant, impatient, and dismissive. Feelings of inadequacy are frequently denied or hidden behind a blustering defensiveness. A scared father arrives at a parent-teacher conference ready to be aggressive. As he announces, "I'll give Brandon's teacher something to think about!" he hides his fears and is utterly unaware of the teacher's. It is hard to imagine he will listen or be listened to.

Vulnerability can stymie listening that is necessary for effective communication. If the professional is aware of her fears, she has to be careful not to be adversely affected by them. She can't act in ways that will hinder honest connection. And, if she is sensitive and sympathetic to her client's fears, she will have a much better chance to hear what is really being said and a firmer hope that she herself will be heard.

Block #2: Conflicting Agendas

On the surface, a professional-client relationship begins with a unique advantage and a common purpose. The client is seeking a specific service; the professional is there to provide it. Yet, each party comes to this encounter with particular needs and expectations, and these can conflict. Julie comes to her spiritual counselor's office expecting to be warmly welcomed and encouraged to talk about problems with her mother. She trusts that she will be respectfully heard, comforted, and supported. Additionally, she hopes to receive an inspiring and helpful message from the Bible.

In the meantime, Julie's counselor arrives a little late for the session with her. He just had a tragic and troubling hospital visit with a young mother of three children who is dying. This counselor greets Julie rather distractedly and is restless when she doesn't quickly come to the point of her visit. When he pushes her to it, Julie is offended. He offers some words that he hopes are comforting. In fact, he intends to get his client to lighten up, to see that her situation could be a whole lot worse. When Julie leaves, he feels slightly agitated. Julie feels hurt and resentful.

John teaches ninth-grade math and prides himself on connecting with all of his students. But when Billy starts asking about a story problem just as three kids in the back start laughing, John doesn't listen carefully. When Billy continues to question his teacher, John cuts him off. No meeting, no learning, no listening. The teacher's need to keep order checkmates Billy's need and desire to listen and learn.

A social worker behind in her casework doesn't want to listen to a client's concern about his missing food stamps. A doctor intends to spend quality time with each patient, wanting to hear about each of their lives as well as their symptoms. However, this physician's best intentions are thwarted by his awareness that he also has eight patients in the waiting room, and five calls to make to insurance companies. A client drives an hour for a meeting with his tax lawyer, and then can't focus on the lawyer's advice because he's distracted by an argument he just had with his wife on the car phone.

Sometimes the professional and the client fail to connect because each has an entirely different expectation for the appointment. The agenda is not the same for each client. Some professionals recall incidents of mismatched agendas:

♦ **Accountant**: "I thought this client really needed to see me right away. She sounded so upset on the phone. I reviewed all of her tax records in preparation for the appointment. It turns out that she really wanted to ask me about her boyfriend's tax return. I'd never even met the guy."

♦ **Physician**: "I put two hours aside to give this patient a full physical. We always start out in my office to identify any concerns—minor or major—and then go into the examining room. It turns out she just wanted to renew her medications."

♦ **Psychologist**: "I'm always surprised when a client wants to spend a whole session telling me a story. A guy I saw recently described his entire trip to Bermuda with his fiancée. Every time I tried to intervene, he would listen a bit, nod his head, and go right on with his story.

I thought he might need to explore how he was relating with his fiancée. He just wanted to talk. The session ended. He said, 'Thanks a lot, Doc. You're great' and left."

Professionals can avoid some frustrations by clarifying the agenda when the appointment is set: "We will be doing a full physical" or "Do you want to review your tax return?" Sometimes the professional needs to abandon his own expectation for the appointment, as the psychologist did. Apparently, the client needed to tell a story that day. On the other hand, expectations and assumptions can get in the way of listening. The professional may assume that he or she knows the "purpose" of the appointment but may not take the time to verify it with the client. Sometimes the professional may not be flexible enough to listen to a new concern from the client.

The professional and client come together in an ideal setting when each is free to focus on his or her purpose. The professional is there to listen to the client and to provide expertise in responding to the client's need. The client comes prepared to be clear about his or her needs and questions, and should then listen carefully to the help offered. This ideal, however, can easily be thwarted by a variety of emotions, pressures, distractions, expectations, and assumptions.

Block #3: Burnout

In general, professionals enter their fields of expertise with high ideals. They want to be the best rabbi, doctor, lawyer, social worker, psychologist, or teacher that they can be. They want to serve their clients with competence, skill, compassion, and dedication. They would proudly claim to be good listeners who are alert to their clients' needs. But professionals suffer from too much stress and pressure. There are too many clients and not enough time. Too much work and not enough play can result in professional fatigue or even burnout. A hospital administrator in the billing department admitted:

I had explained how to read the insurance Explanation of Benefits for the millionth time. It seemed that this patient still wasn't getting it. Frankly, I think she didn't want to get it because then she would have to pay her bill. But even when people don't have a bill to pay, they look at the insurance papers as if they are written in a foreign language. It's just not that difficult. I have no patience anymore. I'm getting jaded. I'm beginning to see all people as stupid or devious.

Professionals from all fields have described the temptation to dismiss a client's uniqueness with a shrug and an unspoken "Here we go again." "I've heard this complaint a thousand times," they mutter to themselves. Instead of listening to this unique individual, the professional becomes blasé and is inclined to assume that he knows what the client is going to say. He makes the awful assumption that he doesn't need to listen. He can lapse into a mindset in which he tells himself, "Just get on with it, give the advice, provide the answer, and get out of the office as soon as possible."

After years of routine pressures, it is easy for any professional to grow arrogant and see little value in listening. After all, he or she is highly educated and has had years of experience. Isn't it better for him or her to talk, and for the client to listen? A study by the American Hospital Association concluded that the most common complaint of patients is that their doctors lacked compassion and failed to listen. Dr. Richard M. Frankel, who conducted the study for the Rochester Medical School, wrote, "Patients would complain that their physicians never looked at them during the entire encounter, made them feel humiliated or used medical jargon that left them confused. "Dr. Frankel, reporting on the study, stated:

Physicians readily assume that the patient's first complaint is the most important. . . . For most patients we've studied, when their physician gives them the chance to say everything on their mind, [it is] their third complaint, on average, [that] is the most troubling.

Doctors can pre-empt communication from their patients. By failing to listen, they might prevent their patients from revealing their most serious symptom. Another study supported the finding from the Rochester Medical School. It analyzed the medical interviews between internists and their patients, revealing that within the first eighteen seconds of the conversation, doctors interrupted as their patients tried to say what was wrong with them.

It is safe to assume that if a similar study were conducted to study clergy members, psychologists, lawyers, and other professionals, the results would be same. In fact, studies by researchers Carkhuff and Berenson focused on listening skills and the other characteristics necessary for a counselor to initiate therapeutic change. The studies revealed that bartenders and other non-trained individuals showed much more empathy than trained therapists (*Sources of Gain in Counseling and Psychotherapy*, Bernard G. Berenson and Robert R. Carkhuff, Holt, Rinehart and Winston, Inc. 1967). Professional training, they found,

Doctors can preempt communication from their patients. By failing to listen, they might prevent their patients from revealing their most serious symptom.

actually seemed to reduce one's ability to listen. Reports on counseling provided to those impacted by the 9/11 terrorist attacks echoed the other studies of professional counselors. The 9/11 victims responded more favorably to peer counseling than to professional services.

Clients can also suffer from too many unsatisfactory experiences with professionals. These disappointing encounters diminish a patient's trust and desire to listen. A forty-three-year-old woman who had diabetes, arthritis, and a heart problem had been seeing many doctors and specialists since she was a small child. She said to us:

I go into a doctor's office with a chip on my shoulder. I've seen the disinterested doctor, the "touchy-feely" one, the "I'm-going-to-get-to-the-bottom-of-your-symptoms" doctor, the ones who think I'm nuts, and the ones who think I'm causing my own problems. Frankly, when the doctor starts to talk I just hear "blah, blah, blah." You would think I would stop going. Actually, I decide after each doctor's visit that I'm never going to step foot into another doctor's office. I have to face it though. I need doctors. There is never going to be a time when I'll be cured. I have to find a better way to listen to them. Who knows? Maybe there will be something worth listening to.

Block #4: Problem-Solving

In the professional-client interaction, one—the client—comes with a problem. The other one—the professional—comes to solve it. Ironically, it is this very dynamic—the problem vs. solution dynamic—that can lead to poor listening in both parties. The expert can so focus on the "problem" that he fails to listen, especially to the client's feelings. These feelings can appear to be irrelevant or even distracting to the problem-solving process. But, if these feelings are not attended to, the professional can thwart his intention to help. The lawyer in this scenario encountered that very problem.

Shortly after her mother died, Eileen decided to have her own will written. She had agonized over a number of issues for years. As a result, she had never completed the will. She explained to her lawyer that one dilemma had to do with her son with Down's syndrome. She wanted to leave sufficient funds for his care. The lawyer then interrupted quickly, explaining, "That's no problem. I've done a lot of these kinds of wills. We can set up a trust. . . ." As he continued to talk, Eileen became distracted. She pictured her son looking inconsolably for her as he tried to go through their morning routine alone. She did not hear the lawyer's solution. For her, finding someone who would care for and love her son was more complex and troubling than the "simpler" task of providing financial support for him.

Had the lawyer "listened" to Eileen and attended to her anxiety over her son's well-being, Eileen would have experienced more of a connection. She could have been more attentive to his legal advice.

All these professionals are busy solving problems, but they are missing the person.

The expert who doesn't listen to the whole person seeking help can be as insensitive as the journalist in this historic but sick joke: "But other than that, Mrs. Lincoln, how did you like the play?" The priest may be too eager to get to the funeral arrangements. The lawyer may be too focused on financial details of the divorce settlement. The doctor might be giving advice prematurely. All these professionals are busy solving problems, but they are missing the person. They might even find themselves solving the wrong problems.

There's also a risk that clients may stop listening when problem solving takes over the professional-client interaction. In this incident, a patient offered a "Yes, but . . ." response typically triggered by his or her own preoccupation with a possible solution.

When Amanda complained to her physician that her stomach was still bothering her, the physician suggested a new medication. She responded, "Yes, I can try that, but I used to take a similar one and it didn't work." When the doctor said, "Well, we have quite a number of drugs we can try," Amanda said, "Yes, I know, but I was thinking maybe we should look at my diet to see if it's causing the pain in some way."

Because the physician has proceeded too quickly to his solution, he does not listen to Amanda's thoughts. She, in turn, does not listen to him. Both could easily be frustrated. Unlike Amanda, some patients and clients will accept an expert's solution without even questioning it. He or she may do this at the cost of denying thoughts and experiences.

Anderson's stockbroker impatiently remarked, "No one can predict the market, of course, but I'm telling you I have a gut feeling that we should unload this stuff now." Anderson reluctantly signed the papers to sell the stock even though his "gut feeling" didn't agree with the broker's. He didn't want to look like the typical client who hired a broker but wouldn't follow his advice. After all, this broker had always commended him for being a "good client." "You're not one of those clients whom I have to practically baby-sit."

The professional must be patient, must listen to the whole person, and not simply concentrate on "the problem." Otherwise, he risks speaking when the other is not listening. He may be trying to solve the problem when the other is not ready for a solution. Or, he may be providing a solution but for the wrong problem. The expert's first task is to hear his client as a person to be met and served, and not a problem to be solved. After his listening, connecting, understanding, and clarifying, then and only then can his services be truly helpful.

Reflection Questions

@ Do you know what to say when you think your doctor (or lawyer, teacher, minister) isn't listening to you?

@ Do you know your agenda when meeting with your doctor, lawyer, counselor?

@ As a professional, can you identify your own symptoms of burnout, a stage where you can no longer listen to others?

CHAPTER FIVE

Managers
and
Employees

People in business organizations have to communicate clearly if they are to reach their basic goal, making a profit. Business managers have to set forth clear objectives and should ensure that they are heard. To lead effectively, it is imperative that executives listen to others in ways that draw from each person's strengths and gifts. Managers can only manage well if they solicit ideas from those they manage, and then listen to these ideas with respect and understanding. Staff members must listen carefully to management so that they are moving in a coordinated and unified direction. When all parts of the organization are connecting, each one is being heard. When trust frees each department and each individual to work at an optimal level, then effective decisions are made, goals are achieved, money is made, and individuals feel satisfied. Again, as

Shakespeare said, "'Tis a consummation devoutly to be wished."

Organizations that value the individual value listening. They know that their success depends on each person working at his or her creative best in coordination with all their coworkers. If each employee trusts that she is recognized, that her views are heard, then she is motivated to contribute in every way that she can. Each worker needs to know that his boss listens to his opinion and values his contribution. Each boss has to be confident that when he speaks, the employees listen and understand.

Such listening facilitates effective decision making. Individuals therefore become free to express themselves, free from the fear of being shot down or ignored. Candor triumphs over silence, clarity over ambiguity, spontaneous expression over insincere manipulation. Thus, decisions can be made that are informed with the honest thoughts and feelings of all individuals. Individuals, in turn, take ownership of decisions in which they feel like full participants. Implementation of goals is ensured in contrast to work settings in which productivity is hampered by an atmosphere that breeds resentment, distrust, and confusion.

Listening also promotes teamwork based on respect for differences. Diversity is celebrated because difference is understood as complementary, not divisive. Those in research can be listened to and appreciated as supportive of sales and not as hindrances. Technical specialists can be partners to marketing personnel. Analysts can team with the creators of new products. Women can work with men, races and ethnic groups can blend. Older workers can complement the younger ones. Listening uncovers valuable common ground underlying differences.

A team is strong when the players and their differences are understood and respected for their contributions. As on a winning football team, the backs understand the importance of the linemen. The quarterback values the center while the defense appreciates the offense. All of these players work together in close coordination, each one playing his part of the team. Understanding promotes appreciation, respect and trust—all key ingredients to an organization's health.

Yet organizations can be like dysfunctional families. Listening, and the trust that it fosters, can disappear. When it does, paranoia, cynicism, deceit, apathy, power struggles, turf wars, posturing, hostility, and tension poison the atmosphere, abort the organization's goals, and make life miserable for all organization members. We spend much of our lives at work. When the workplace is healthy, we feel better, work better, live better. What prevents organizations of all kinds from becoming places where listening and mutual trust can thrive? Listening blocks that occur frequently in business settings are outlined in the next section.

Blocks to Effective Listening

Block #1: Competition

Competition can be good, stimulating top performance, bringing out the best in each individual. It becomes destructive and a block to attentive listening when one employee's success comes at the cost of another's. In business, individuals need to work together for the common goal. They need to trust that not only is each employee working at optimal level for the success of the whole organization, but also that coworkers have a stake in each employee's personal success. Competition turns ugly when individuals step on one another, hurt one another, or even ignore one another in order to succeed. When someone's accomplishment is viewed as a threat, teamwork collapses. In this dysfunctional setting, the motto "He wins, I lose" replaces "One wins, we all win."

Following the football analogy, the ugly competitive thinking becomes, "If he scores, I look bad." A great run is met not with high-fives but with resentment and jealousy. Inevitably, the conclusion is reached: "Next time I won't block for him. He'll see how good he looks then." From playing as teammates to win, they become enemies—each man for himself. In that atmosphere everyone loses. An insurance agent describes the effect of such divisive behavior in his workplace:

> I was so pumped after my interviews for this job. It seemed to fit all the things I wanted in a job: lots of room for growth, lots of ways to prove myself, and a great atmosphere. The people seemed pretty nice, at least the ones I met. It has been a shock to discover that they are so territorial about their clients. The first day I asked the woman in the cubicle next to me if I could take a look at how she organized her client files. She said, "No, you have to find your own way." A couple of months later, I went to share some information that I had gotten about this other guy's client and my partner had a fit. He said, "Keep it to yourself. Don't be spending your time helping them out. They wouldn't do it for you and we can probably use that information to our benefit." I finally realized how this place operates.

Lack of cooperation is rampant in many organizations. Self-interest triumphs over teamwork. "What's in it for me?" becomes the criterion for action. No one wants to consider, "What is the plan of action that best meets the firm's goals?" This mindset arises from self-focus over team focus. Some companies try to combat this attitude by teaching employees that whenever they receive data from an outside source they should ask themselves, "Who would profit most from this information?" In effect the question prompts workers to consider the information and match it with their knowledge of the needs and goals of people on their team. Unless workers are aware of one another, listen to each other, know the type of work, objectives, and needs of their fellow workers, they can't pass along pertinent information even when good intentions are present. Sharing information freely is one sign of effective teamwork. It's a sign that team members have listened to each other.

It is common that employees treat one another as impersonal work units. They fail to know their coworkers or appreciate their concerns, goals, hopes, and fears. Roger Strauss III told us that while editing *Carrying the Fire*, a book written by astronaut Michael Collins, he mentioned to Collins that he hadn't talked about what he and fellow astronauts Neil Armstrong and Buzz Aldrin had learned about each other. Collins responded, "There's nothing to report. We didn't talk except about our separate tasks on board." Three men alone in space who were trained in technical thinking and space flight! They didn't share their thoughts or feelings on their way to the moon!

> It is common that employees treat one another as impersonal work units.

In a more down-to-earth example, a sensitive man with an important position in a large shipping firm shared his disappointment at receiving a poor performance review. He had presumed that his boss would have known about his difficult divorce and taken this stressful situation into account. Team members need to know the factors that are influencing one another at work. People truly interested in building a smoothly functioning team are open to their coworkers. They listen and offer support where it is needed.

A New York policeman noted that the entire police force was affected deeply by the devastation of the 9/11 terrorist attack on the World Trade Center. Because of that shared sadness in police personnel around him, he paid closer attention to a couple of fellow cops in his department. He said he thought that they were already in rough spots in their lives and "I kept my eye on them in case they couldn't handle it."

When we, as Community Psychological Consultants, consult with a company, we encourage team building at offsite workshops. In a new setting, individuals can learn to listen to others' interests and goals, their needs at work, and the challenges that they encounter there. We suggest weekly meetings in their departments where they are encouraged to listen to their peers and are invited to discuss current projects and objectives. The focus is growth in awareness of and trust in their colleagues at work. Competitiveness that turns ugly has the opposite effect. It breeds a climate where people are guarded and separated from one another. Excessive competitiveness is the enemy of trust, understanding, and productivity.

Block #2: Fear

In the chapter on professional and client relationships, the fear of bad news is identified as a deterrent to a client's calm effective listening. In the business world, fear is endemic. It's part of the territory. The fear of being fired or passed over for promotion is accompanied by the fear of failure, the fear of not getting a raise or a bonus, and the fear of disappointing the boss. These fears are natural. They are consequences of the fact that, in most organizations, our fate and fortune are not solely in our hands. We depend on others who have power to dispense or withhold promotions, opportunities, and even financial well-being. The challenge is to admit our fears, dispel obsessions triggered by fears, and learn how to listen in spite of them.

A highly successful banker who has been promoted frequently and who heads a major division in one of the world's largest banks is constantly afraid that he will be "found out," exposed as inadequate despite the fact that he is highly competent. Whenever his boss calls, he's sure that he will hear criticism, even the news that he's being fired. He told us, "You can't imagine how hard it is for me to relax and listen to what he is telling me. I am waiting for the bomb to drop."

This banker's fears are extreme. On a smaller scale, real fears about how a superior is evaluating your job performance is an everyday experience, and makes listening difficult. A manager might simply wish to offer constructive criticism to an employee about the way she is performing at a job. That's part of the job for a responsible manager. But the recipient might feel especially vulnerable and might fail to hear the helpful observations. Instead of hearing a suggestion about prioritizing tasks, the employee might sense that her boss thinks she's stupid. Instead of hearing that some public speaking classes could be advantageous for him, a defensive employee often reads a different message from the suggestion. Suggestions about taking a class or changing the way he does something is misread as personal criticism. A senior executive at a newly merged advertising agency was keenly aware of paranoia at his office. He talked about his reluctance to announce some restructuring of accounts.

I have had these changes in mind for weeks, but I'm so sure that the moves will be misinterpreted that I keep putting off announcing the changes. So many of the people working here are so afraid of losing an account or losing face. They won't appreciate what I am trying to accomplish.

Once again, fear can impede the ability to listen.

Even success can breed fear. Maybe you or your company won't be able to sustain that high level of accomplishment. Once again, fear can impede the ability to listen. Serena, a crackerjack in sales at a fashion magazine, completed a major sale of advertising space. She told us that she feared she was a "Johnny One Note" and would not be able to duplicate her achievement. In her fear, she couldn't take the teasing albeit complimentary remarks that referred to her success. "When are you going to take over the Northeast division?" her peers joked, offering an affectionate compliment. These compliments only added to her anxieties about performance. Like the tortured, successful banker, Serena lives with the fear that she will be found lacking. Fears often get in the way of hearing praise.

Sometimes listening to what a boss wants provokes fears about taking a certain action. This fear can prevent listening. Chester holds a high-level management position. Due to his company's merger with a smaller firm, he was told by his boss to fire a subordinate colleague whom his boss never liked. Chester feared delivering the dreadful news. Each time his boss brought up the need to fire the employee, Chester made a brief defense of her and turned the talk to other business. At no time in his procrastination did Chester stop to listen to the reasons his boss gave for wanting to take action. It is easy to stop listening when we fear that a message will ask us to do a difficult job.

Fear is part of doing business—fear of failure, fear of demotion, fear about job security. These fears can impel us to grow in self-confidence and to grow more accomplished in what we do. We can learn to channel the anxiety into positive motivation. We can prevent it from hampering our ability to listen calmly, communicate effectively, and work productively.

Block #3: Judgments

Teamwork in business breaks down when judging and labeling replaces respect and understanding. Division and lack of cooperation result when an individual or a group is written off as "lazy," "arrogant," "self-serving," "stupid." When that type of characterization is prevalent, there is a cessation of efforts to understand a particular person or department. It is easier to brand a person than it is to really understand him. Usually, the consequence of such labeling is further distancing, more distrust, and more labeling. At times, and in subtle ways, this judgmental dynamic reduces collaboration and productivity.

As consultants, we have had the pleasure of assisting many organizations in learning how to function as a team. For us, two companies particularly stand out for their efforts to stop judgments that were poisoning the culture of their companies and handicapping their effectiveness in their markets.

We were asked for help by an oil company in Louisiana that was badly divided between employees involved in oil operations (the "oil men") and those responsible for financial matters ("the bankers").

The men and women on the oil side of the business were primarily from Texas and Louisiana, and tended to be lean, neatly dressed, and slightly taciturn. The "bankers" for the most part had their roots in the Northeast, and were rounder, louder, and more flashily dressed. The oil men who worked "9 to 5" were judged as less committed to the firm. The bankers seldom got out of the building before 7:00 p.m. and frequently stayed much later. The oil men, in turn, wrote off the bankers as a fast-talking, long-lunching crowd that couldn't be fully trusted. Each side needed the other in order to be successful. Without money, they couldn't dig oil wells; without oil, they couldn't make a profit. Nonetheless, the habitual back-and-forth criticizing and labeling kept these two groups from working effectively together.

When they were able to listen to each other in a series of offsite workshops, each group got to know the other's values, feelings, and needs. Then, a mutual respect and understanding knocked down walls of prejudice. Oil men came to realize how authentic many of the bankers were. They saw how genuinely dedicated they were to their families, and how fully committed they were to living spiritual lives. Bankers soon dropped their prejudice toward the "9 to 5" oil men. They learned to appreciate the no-nonsense breed of men and women who worked just as hard as they did, albeit at different hours. Genuine appreciation of the other group's differences and the enjoyment of its similarities eventually replaced negativity and tension. Interaction at work replaced distance, and cross-culture friendships developed. Laughter and good-natured teasing flourished where tension had simmered. The company's profits boomed until a larger firm bought it out. Ten years after the buyout, an anniversary was attended by nearly all of the former employees. The atmosphere was festive. It would not have been easy for a stranger to tell the oil men from the bankers. They were still united. The former CFO wrote to us after the party, "You really helped us to make this a happy and highly productive company and your legacy is intact because so many of our people are leading happy and productive lives using the skills you taught us, especially improved listening and communication."

The second company that stands out for us is a major banking and investment corporation. We worked with the European branch of a bank whose central office is in

London. The judgments that were divisive were primarily between sales and traders. Sales personnel were university graduates. Traders on the whole had not received nearly as much formal education. Those in sales spoke with different accents than the traders, frequently had lunch out of the office with clients, and had different cultural interests, even read different newspapers. A trader we interviewed had a shaved head and played rugby on weekends. He spoke for many of his peers when he described sales,

> *They're too bloody posh to speak to us unless they are on us about a trade. They don't bother me. I pay no attention to them. They're out half of the time at expensive meals. We're busting our tails and they're coasting.*

Sales people meanwhile viewed traders as moody and difficult. As one person put it,

> *It's rather ridiculous. I can't speak to N., the head trader. He literally will not respond when I speak to him about a trade. I stand there looking foolish waiting for him to speak, which he doesn't.*

Each group kept to itself and avoided the other. The traders often went to a pub for beers after work where they'd joke and laugh about sales.

Both groups participated in an offsite workshop where they were challenged to listen to the backgrounds, expectations, and goals that members of each group had. Both sides described the perceptions they held of each other, and gradually shared the hurts and frustrations inflicted by insensitive and prejudiced behaviors. A tough-looking trader was discovered to be a dedicated son to an ill father. A haughty looking head of sales revealed his shyness and awkwardness in groups. Soon these energetic, very smart young men and women were enjoying one another's differences and respecting one another's gifts. The head trader told us, "I'd felt defensive. I thought they [the people in sales, were looking down on me. So, I kept a wall up. I'm easy now. I go out of my way to say 'Hello.' The two groups really do get on now."

Block #4: Lack of Time

As we have mentioned before, the most common objection to listening is, "We don't have time!" Spouses, professionals, parents feel the pressure of competing demands and report that they just are not able to take the time to listen. People in business make the same complaint. Listening is often perceived as a luxury. It's fine, they all say, when you have time to do it, but not really practical in the rush of daily life at home and certainly not at work. We've been told by people in business, "It would be nice to focus on listening at meetings, but there simply isn't time for that. The meetings go on too long as it is."

The consequences of not listening, however, are an incredible waste of time, a waste of money, and a waste of human energy. When a waitress doesn't listen carefully to an order, the steak may arrive well done, not rare. The steak is wasted, so is the chef's time and that of the waitress and the patron. An assistant doesn't listen to the specifications regarding the fifty binders he is to prepare. As a result, fifty flawed binders are produced that have to be discarded.

> The consequences of not listening, however, are an incredible waste of time, a waste of money, and a waste of human energy.

What a waste of paper, a waste of the assistant's time, and a waste of his emotional energy as he scrambles to create another fifty binders in time for the meeting. Every day in business, time and materials are wasted due to poor listening.

The owner of a tool manufacturing company admitted, "You wouldn't believe the waste of material each month! It hurts our profit margin if foremen don't get the specifications of an order clear. They are rushing too much to listen and, for God's sake, to take accurate notes." He asked in frustration, "Can you teach them that?"

Listening in business is often a simple act of clarification that does not require much time, simply some skill. A worker can confirm that he has heard clearly by saying back to his boss, "Do I have it clear? You want the numbers on the contract proposal by Friday, and you want a list of potential candidates for participation on the diversity committee by March 1?" Checking briefly to see if you have heard directions, information, or requests by repeating them back saves time, it doesn't waste it. A hairdresser told us, "I always listen to the client for a while and then I say, 'Let me make sure I know what you want.' Saves a lot of heartache."

Sending a memo after a meeting, outlining the decisions that were made allows participants to amend or confirm the meeting's outcome. These are simple listening responses that guarantee that individuals are clearly understanding one another and moving in the same, agreed upon direction. In other words, this kind of listening is certainly not wasting time or money, and not causing heartache.

People in business say that they have no time to listen, but they sit through endless meetings that go nowhere because no one is really listening. Participants in these meetings tend to repeat themselves since they have no assurance that they have really been heard. Other people "go off" on tangents, but no one listens to what they are trying to get at. Still other personnel argue against a point or block a decision because no one heard the resentment they've been harboring since the last meeting. Then another meeting is called since the last one couldn't resolve the issues. More meetings, more time wasted due to a lack of the connection and understanding that listening would have provided. Yet, the same people who suffer through these meetings will complain, "We just don't have the time to get into listening."

Feelings in business are often not heard. One impatient manager snapped, "My God, if we start listening to feelings, we'll never get anything done. We've got a job to do." He's right about having a job to do; wrong if he thinks that that job can be done while ignoring feelings. A worker who is angry and disappointed at his annual compensation might be the same worker who is often late for meetings, is taking sick days, and resists taking on more responsibility. An executive we counseled was not included in several high-level strategy sessions that would affect his department. When he tried to express his frustration, he was offered a few clichés that were supposed to reassure him. No one listened to his concerns. He told us, "I've had it! They cut you out, don't want to hear from you. Then they expect you to work like crazy for them!" His frustration and resentment at not being heard are definitely affecting his attitude and will most likely affect his performance. People need to be heard when they feel confused, hurt, disappointed, and angry as well as when they have feelings of great satisfaction. Managers who do not take the time to listen are not taking advantage of the opportunity to recognize, encourage, and comfort. They are neglecting their roles as motivators.

Listening is an investment in individuals. It demonstrates interest. When a manager listens, he hears the needs of the employees so that he or the company can meet them. Listening helps the boss identify the strengths of his workers and provides him with ideas on how best to employ them. Listening uncovers weaknesses and opens the possibility of correcting them. It hears confusion in employees and presents the opportunity to clarify and provide direction.

A previously frustrated accountant reported with relief, "I finally got my boss to listen to me. I was going out of my mind with boredom doing what I've been doing for years. I needed a new direction. He's given me a new area of responsibility and even provided some technical coaching I needed. It's a whole new ball game." The accountant is recharged, ready to accomplish new goals for himself and for his company.

Listening uncovers weaknesses and opens the possibility of correcting them.

Reflection Questions

@ When (time or circumstances) do you fail to listen well on the job?

@ Think of someone in your organization who listens well. Can you describe what he or she does that leads you to feel heard?

@ What would you do to make more time for listening at work?

CHAPTER SIX

Friends
and
Siblings

A h, these are the relationships in which we can relax, trusting that we can listen and be heard, free from the agendas that can impede empathy in other relationships. Interactions between friends and siblings can present their own set of challenges, but there is often freedom from some of the intensity and responsibility that can characterize other relationships.

You can listen to your friend without having to guide and protect as you do in your role as a parent. A sibling relationship or a friendship doesn't mean having to resolve problems or have them resolved as in a professional-client interaction. And the rapport and exchange with a friend or sibling doesn't come with the intense emotion that can prevent you from listening to your spouse. With your friends or siblings, you don't have the responsibility to impose limits and rules. You don't have the task of solving problems. You don't have to make decisions regarding household finances, and you don't have to fear that you might be fired.

We are free of the distractions and hurdles of other relationships. The pressures and constraints put on communication is lifted. With a friend, brother or sister, you can let down your hair or your guard. You can trust that you are going to be heard in whatever you are trying to say. The author Dinah Craik described the sensation,

Oh, the comfort

The inexpressible comfort

Of feeling safe with a person

Having neither to weigh thoughts,

Nor measure words

But pouring them

All right out—just as they are,

Chaff and grain together,

Certain that a faithful hand will

Take and sift them

And with the breath of kindness

Blow the rest away.

Your spouse might be too threatened to hear about a temptation to be unfaithful, but your friend will listen. Your parent would be too wounded to hear about your problems at home or at work, but your friend will understand. You might not want to say what you're thinking to your boss, spouse, or client. But you're safe "unloading" on a brother or sister who has known you all your life.

Siblings know so much about the past that influences you now. For instance, they might understand your feeling of inferiority. They had the same critical father. They know instinctively when you are afraid, impatient, or hurt. They were connecting to you in these emotions when you were four, eight, and twelve years old. When you express your attitudes toward God, the government, or the world in general, brothers and sisters "get it." Their attitudes were formed in the same setting. We often don't have to say much to a brother or sister; he or she has been there and understands. A young woman poignantly described the experience.

When my sister came into my hospital room after I lost my baby after three miscarriages, she just scooped me into her arms. She knew, without my having to say a word, what losing a baby meant for me. She knew that I liked to be the mother when we played house when we were little girls. She knew how I had talked about having six children from the time I was in my early teens. And she knew how Mike and I talked about having a big family when we got married. She knew that I had never wanted to have a career—that my dream had always been to be a mother.

If we are fortunate, we have friends who have known us for many years, through many ages and stages. When you describe a feeling or event today, your friends can hear you because they've been with you through similar emotions and experiences in the past. Adam and Stephen have been friends for years—since they went to Columbia together. When Adam described a blowup he had with a broker in a rival firm, Stephen explained why he was able to simply listen:

Adam is a great guy and he's brilliant. You can always depend on him to tell the truth. But he has no tolerance for people who don't think as fast as he does, and his anger explodes like a rocket. It will settle down just as fast, but you have to be prepared to weather it. I can do that because I have weathered it many times. I know he'll be fine later. Unfortunately, not everyone knows him as well as I do, and his anger alienates a lot of people.

Friends can be even safer confidants than siblings. Unlike our brothers and sisters, we are able to choose our friends. We tend to form friendships with those who share our interests and activities. In general, it is easy to hear one another. We agree on a lot of things. On a building project for Habitat for Humanity, a friend remarked, "I love doing this with you. I know you understand why I need to do this work."

Yet, despite the ease of communication between good friends and siblings, listening can still suffer. There are plenty of times when friends and siblings do not listen and are not listened to in return. Consciously or unconsciously, we can even stop trying to make the more profound connections that listening could facilitate. We develop patterns of behavior with our siblings and friends that can diminish the prospect of really being heard. Despite the ease and familiarity between us, listening can still suffer. We need to be alert to the threats and blocks to effective listening that can exist even in such potentially close and comforting relationships. There are common blocks to listening that are encountered in relationships with friends and siblings.

Blocks to Effective Listening

Block #1: Perpetuating Roles

We develop roles in our family of origin such as peacemaker, comedian, good girl or good boy, rebel, responsible one. We often continue to play these roles with siblings and friends. The roles can block our ability to listen or to be heard. If we get attention for being funny, for knowing how to make everyone laugh at the dinner table, then being the comedian becomes our claim to fame. It defines our identity and predicts our behavior. No matter how tense or awkward the situation might be, "Benny will crack us up." So if a sibling or a friend is attempting to communicate sadness or fear, Benny can't listen. He's supposed to make us laugh. Benny may not be able to share or be heard in his own times of sorrow. He is trapped in the funnyman role.

If Jeremy, who always responds as peacemaker and comforter to any member of the family, tries to voice his anger or sadness, no one is prepared to listen. A woman describes the reaction of her husband's siblings after her husband became depressed and was hospitalized.

I can't believe how his sister and brothers are reacting. They are paralyzed. One of his brothers hasn't even visited him in the hospital. His sister does visit, but she still asks him for advice and won't talk to him about his depression. This is so weird. He has been there for all of them, but they don't know what to do to be there for him.

Someone who always acted as a sage or counselor will probably continue to give advice and information to her friends rather than listening to them. The "bad boy-tough guy" cannot offer a compassionate ear. The "sweet girl" cannot hear or be heard in anger. Role-playing is a way of getting stuck in a predictable and expected way of behaving. You might be naturally funny, but in your assigned role, you are expected to play the comedian all the time. We might be blessed with generous spirits, but this assigned role may demand that we act constantly as givers,

> Role-playing is a way of getting stuck in a predictable and expected way of behaving.

leaving us drained and frustrated. Likewise, the successful one of the family is not allowed to fail. Carl, the first college graduate from a large family, complained to us, "I'm not going home for Christmas this year. My grandparents will be there, and I know they will not let go of the fact that I haven't gotten a job yet. They'll bring up the topic anywhere and everywhere, and are oblivious to the anxiety I feel."

Old hurts from childhood, for example, can block listening when they surface in a conversation. Nancy's sister sometimes cannot listen to Nancy despite their affection for each other.

I love my sister and I love to talk with her. There is one area, though, that we have to avoid. I will always resent the fact that my grandmother decided very early in our lives that I was the smart one, and my sister was the pretty one. Wherever we went, she would introduce us by saying, "Here's my beauty and here's my brain." So, if my sister starts talking with fondness about our summers with my grandmother, I just clam up. I think that was a terrible thing to do to two little girls, but my sister doesn't see it that way. She says my grandmother was just being affectionate.

Roles can block full expression of true feelings and can block the ability to hear them. Roles are static; real life is not. For example, Karen is usually tough, but not always. Laying aside the tough role, she can also occasionally be gentle, unsure of herself, and needy. She has a right and a need to be herself, and a right to be heard in all her dimensions. Role-playing can scuttle that experience. Benny is funny, but he is more than a funnyman. Sam is serious but not always. Friendship and sibling relationships that can be so rewarding and freeing can also become stifling because behaviors are scripted for roles established long ago. We heard two women planning a party. One said, "Make sure we include Nancy. She'll keep it lively." What room does Nancy have to play a different role with these friends, other than being "lively" at the party? We might do well to list our closest friends and then ask ourselves what we expect from them. We could also ask ourselves what we think they expect from us. It is very easy to slip into roles with expectations that can strangle the freedom to be yourself.

Block #2: Wearing Two Hats

The caring and listening that friendships provide can be threatened when these friendships spill over into a professional-client realm. When a friend is also a doctor, lawyer, real-estate agent, minister, or other professional, communication and its listening dimension can be strained. Tara, a real-estate agent, might not have any difficulty hearing Kim talk about her frustration at sellers overpricing their homes, but how well could she listen if she were currently selling Kim's house? Carter would probably listen sympathetically to Ron rant and rave about wives ripping off the husbands they are divorcing if he were not a divorce lawyer. Arlene listens as carefully as she can when she's wearing her physician's white jacket and sitting in her office. She might not want to listen at all, however, when her friend Jane begins to describe her daughter's cough while they are shopping in Macy's. Wearing two hats is fine, but trying to wear them at the same time can be awkward and burdensome.

For the professional to listen well to a friend, she or he first needs to clarify what hat to wear. Will this conversation be an exchange between friends or a professional consultation? Does this friend expect empathy or professional advice, or both? A money manager told us how he tries to keep things clear. "Whenever friends start to talk about money outside my office, I interrupt pretty quickly and tell them I can't talk about this unless I'm in my office with all the facts in front of me. Of course sometimes people get offended as though I'm accusing them of trying to get free advice, but most of the time they understand and move on." A mother of three children who is also a child psychiatrist told us how she tries to distinguish expectations.

I try to make it clear to all my friends that I don't want to be put in that awful position of advising treatment for someone who is not actually my patient. What if I made a mistake? But I have one friend whom I really cherish, who inevitably brings up something about her child who is autistic. I'm never really sure if she needs me to hear what she is saying as a doctor or as a very loving friend. I'm not sure if she knows. It's not easy to keep the lines clear.

It is not easy for the professional to know in what capacity he or she is being addressed. It is not easy to set boundaries as the money manager did. The professional friend doesn't want to offend or appear haughty. Yet, until she is clear about the intention and need of her friend, she will be hard-pressed to know how to respond. Should she listen without any other agenda? Should she listen in a way that clarifies the issue? Should she offer expert advice? Only when she knows what her friend wants will she know how to respond appropriately and compassionately.

The two-hat phenomenon complicates the friendship not only for the professional but also for the other person. Jane's daughter's health monopolizes her thoughts even while she is looking at shoes in Macy's. She wants to talk freely with her friend, but will Arlene think that she is being asked for some free professional advice? Will Arlene think she is being used? Will she say something critical about the way Jane is caring for her daughter? With another friend Jane would be free of these fears. Friendship should provide a grand opportunity to speak freely and to be clearly heard. Yet, the fact that a friend is a professional can hinder communication. An acquaintance told us, "I've played golf almost every Wednesday for eight years with Father Ed. He's a good guy, but I'm careful what I say. I don't want to offend him, and I don't want him to preach to me. We keep pretty much to golf."

Having friends who are experts or working in a field very different from yours can be stimulating. It can add some interesting dimensions to this friendship. The knowledge, expertise, and different experiences of these friends typically commands your respect, as do their accomplishments. They have a particular view of life and events that's formed by their education, work, travel and the people they've met. These friendships can be wonderfully broadening. Being alert to the potential downside of such friendships can help to protect their rich potential.

Block #3: Being Loyal

One of the gifts of friendship is loyalty. Others might let you down, even your minister or boss, but not a friend, brother, or sister! We hope and trust that these special people will always be in our corner, will always be on our side.

The most moving moment in the classic movie *It's a Wonderful Life* is the scene in which all the townspeople loyal to the James Stewart character put their small savings into his bank to assure its survival. We cherish the loyalty of friendship whether we're observing it or receiving it. We are deeply hurt by the absence of it, by betrayal. A poignant moment in another classic movie, *On the Waterfront*, occurs when the character portrayed by Marlon Brando faces his brother who has betrayed him and ruined his boxing career. "I could have been a contender," Brando tells him. "You shoulda taken care of me." We can all resonate with the hurt of being betrayed by a brother.

Nonetheless, the very loyalty that a good friend or sibling gives can become an impediment to honest, careful listening. When someone is expressing anger or frustration about your friend, your loyal defense of your friend can stop you from listening to the speaker and the feelings. When a friend is talking about how fed up he is with his boss, in loyalty you might jump in with support and advice for that friend. "Tell him what you really think of him," you will say, instead of listening to the message beneath the emotions. Your agenda includes showing your friend that you are in your friend's corner. That personal "prejudice" can distract you from listening to and hearing what your friend is actually experiencing.

Commiseration is a common expression of friendship that tries to show solidarity. It's a flawed substitute for listening. Tanya, for instance, often complains about men. "They don't know what to do with feelings. They all run when you say anything that looks like you are getting close to a feeling." Her friend Emily, anxious to support Tanya, joins in. "Oh, my God, you've got that right. Don't even try to talk about what you feel. They wouldn't have a clue."

These two can easily egg each other on to more complaints, more judgments, and more gripes about emotionally clueless men. Emily probably thinks that she has been loyal to Tanya and that she has listened to her. But Emily has probably not heard the real feelings that are prompting Tanya's criticisms. In fact, she might simply be disappointed in her boyfriend, hurt by something he said, lonely that he is not confiding in her, frustrated that he did not understand how a behavior of his affected her. Emily didn't take the time to listen. She showed support by piling on to Tanya's condemnation of men.

Misery might love company, but, more than the company, individuals need a safe place to be truly heard. Jason and Seth lost their jobs at the same time and decided to job hunt together. Initially, their plan to buoy each other up and share job search ideas was a great idea. But as the weeks went by, their interactions were more often gripe sessions that grew increasingly depressing for both of them. When Seth would say, "This job market stinks; there are no jobs anywhere," Jason would echo him with, "We've tried everything. The jobs just aren't there." If Jason would say, "I'm thinking of giving up on the search. Maybe I'm just not meant to be employed," Seth would chime in, "Me, too. We're part of a whole generation that's going to be unemployed." Instead of genuinely listening to the fear, discouragement, and helplessness that each felt while looking for a job, and instead of sticking to the plan to energize each other, they fell into the trap of mutual commiseration.

Listening, when practiced skillfully, is a profound way to communicate loyalty. What better way to express support than to convey real understanding? What better way to show that you are in your friend's corner than to empathize fully with all that she or he is experiencing?

Block #4: Entering the Non-Confrontation Zone

Friendship is often our safest relationship, the place where we can find peace. "My kids are driving me crazy, my boss is on my case at work, my wife is mad at me, but I've got a friend who doesn't hassle me." A good friend can be that guaranteed port in a storm, that bridge over troubled waters. A lack of tension and confrontation are blessings that often come with a good friendship. We so need this no-stress zone that we protect it sometimes at the cost of honest expression and a genuine effort to listen.

Friends and siblings can so avoid tension and confrontation that entire areas of life can be cordoned off from discussion. If a friend drinks too much, then talk of drinking could spur anger, defensiveness, and denial. In wanting peace at all costs, candid sharing disappears. So does listening. At the same time, if that friend did report that she had been involved in a fender-bender on her way home from lunch, we might want to scream, "You've got to stop drinking and get into AA!" Concern about her drinking could prevent us from hearing her embarrassment or humiliation about being in an accident.

If religion is an area that friends have mutually, but tacitly, chosen to avoid discussing, then they can't share feelings or thoughts related to this topic. Louise said sadly, "My best friend left our congregation a long time ago. I want to tell her how much I like our new minister, but I can just hear her scorning me for still belonging to this church." Louise can't share and her friend can't

> Friendship is often our safest relationship, the place where we can find peace.

listen. Their mutual fear of confrontation is outweighing a sense that they could discuss topics they don't agree on. A woman told us, "It's sad, but I can't tell my siblings who I voted for in the election. They would react so emotionally; it's not worth it." So, those closest to her don't hear the feelings, thoughts, and values that are very meaningful to her. Peace at all costs in close relationships often comes at a very high price indeed.

The distance and alienation that results from making certain topics taboo can also develop between friends whose circumstances change dramatically.

With siblings and with most friends, we have a lot in common. We might share the fact that we are single or middle-class, Midwesterners or Protestant. Tension—or a distancing—can occur if one person gets married, becomes wealthy, moves away, or converts to another religion. One woman could not see a way to close the gap that had developed between her and a childhood friend.

My best friend's husband lost his job two and a half years ago. Until then, we sent our children to the same private school—from preschool to the fourth grade. Even though he just got a new job, they really can't afford to send their children to the same school any more. If I talk about a problem I'm having with a teacher, I can just feel her stiffen. I understand that it's painful for her. She loved it when her children went to this school. I would love to talk to her about it, but she won't talk to anyone—especially me—about the change in her financial circumstances. I really need someone to listen to me about these problems that my daughter is having in school. This separation is straining our friendship.

Neither of these women is willing to confront the issue of their changed circumstances. They simply avoid certain topics, and neither is heard in her fear, inadequacy, and self-doubt. As a result, their friendship may be weakened or even lost. As individuals grow and as their lives develop, they might become incompatible with former friends. In life, there are necessary losses. But there are many other relationships that could be saved and transformed by honest communication.

Reflection Questions

@ What role do you sometimes "play" that prevents you from listening well?

@ Are there any topics that you are reluctant to discuss with a friend because you don't believe that he or she will hear you?

@ Can you identify the differences in your behavior when you're simply being loyal and sympathetic, and when you're really listening?

PART TWO

So Many Ways

Not to Listen

Yakety yak. Don't talk back.

—"Yakety Yak"

sung by The Coasters
Words and music by
Jerry Leiber and Mike Stoller

CHAPTER SEVEN

The Basic Forms
of
Non-Listening

So far, we have depicted the importance and the difficulty of listening in life's key relationships. We have shown that listening is painfully lacking in settings and in interactions where it is deeply needed. Now, it is time to present listening skills and ways to acquire and develop them.

The first step to becoming a good listener is to be aware of the ways that you do not listen. Can you identify your own behaviors that "pass" for listening? They are poor substitutes for the behavior that actually hears what's said and conveys understanding to the person who is speaking. Until you realize you have some non-listening habits— despite your best intentions—you will often not listen. Until you identify your non-listening behaviors and learn to check them, you will not become a good listener. Some of these non-listening behaviors that commonly substitute for listening are:

+ Defending
+ "Me too" identifying
+ Advice giving
+ Judging the speaker

We will demonstrate that while these behaviors might seem like genuine listening behaviors, they are not. Some of them will rather easily be unmasked as blatant actions that meet *your need* rather than meet the *speaker's need* to be heard. Some are more subtle expressions of non-listening. All can have a costly or painful impact on the speaker and on your relationship. The sad fact is that very often you are probably reacting to your partner, your child, your client, or your student in a non-listening way. Listening, in brief, demands that the listener:

Focus: The listener focuses on the one speaking, not on him or herself.

Attend: The listener focuses on the information, the feelings, or the message that is being conveyed by the speaker.

Confirm: The listener "checks out," confirms, with the speaker that what he or she has heard is what the speaker is intending to convey.

Despite complaints from those who know us best, most of us consider ourselves to be good listeners. We don't recognize our own failure to listen. So, we are not very motivated to learn what we're not convinced we don't know. We are, however, usually quite aware that others don't listen to us. We would love to tell our boss what we are thinking, needing, and feeling, but we're not sure that he or she would listen. We imagine, instead, that we would be met with an argument, defensiveness, or polite patronizing. These behaviors do not communicate understanding and don't encourage communication.

You would love to be able to share your feelings of loneliness, frustration, hurt, or disappointment with your spouse. Such expression could be so liberating if you were confident that your husband or wife would respond with a genuine effort to understand. Sometimes, instead, you might expect an angry, self-justifying reaction that backfires on you, bringing criticism or blame. So, you keep quiet, withdraw, or blow up at a later date. On some level, you are sadly aware that you're just not being heard. You can't help noticing that the one you most want to listen to you responds instead by defending, arguing, blaming, advising, or pays little or no attention to what you are saying. We know the value of listening by painfully experiencing its absence.

We know the value of listening by painfully experiencing its absence.

You want to be understood for who you are and what you are trying to communicate. Maybe, if you stopped to reflect, you would see that your boss, your spouse, your child, your employee also want you to listen, pay attention, and understand. When you recognize that these central people in your life want to be heard as much as you do, you might be ready to see that just as you are not heard, you do not listen. Just as those close to us don't know how to listen, neither do we.

Your boss seems distracted when you want her to pay attention to you. But, you are also often distracted when your employee, child, or spouse tries to talk to you. Your spouse starts *defending* as soon as you begin to talk, just as you do when he or she talks. Your child offers *excuses*; so do you. Your friend says *"me too"* and immediately tells her story when you are trying to tell yours. That's what you do when a friend narrates an exciting or sad incident. Your father is quick to give *advice* when you try to report difficult feelings. In this same way, you tell others what they should or shouldn't do. When people practice these behaviors, they can seem so natural, and perhaps even caring. The same behaviors, when directed at us, can frustrate and annoy us. They put us on the defensive and discourage us from saying what we think or feel. These behaviors are not efforts to listen, to understand, or "to get into our shoes." *They are non-listening behaviors.* We don't like to receive them. Nor do other people. Not being listened to shuts us down, pushes us away, and makes us think twice before speaking. Instead of connecting us in a safe and trusting way with a boss, spouse, friend, parent, or child, these non-listening behaviors cause distance and alienation between people.

We don't listen, not because we don't care about the speaker or because we're not interested. We don't listen because we have developed non-listening habits, behaviors that are learned and automatic. We probably grew up in a non-listening atmosphere. We might occasionally have had the pleasure of being heard and really understood by a parent or grandparent, teacher or relative. Much of the time, however, we were probably recipients of other behaviors: answers, lectures, warnings, advice, encouraging or discouraging words, and judgments of all kinds. We came, we saw, and we imitated.

We don't listen because we never learned how. We grow up speaking English if that is the language of our parents and classmates. We speak with the accent that we've heard in the family. So, we also communicate, like it or not, in the manner that we learned at home. In order to learn to be an effective listener, we must first heighten our awareness of the non-listening behaviors that we learned and use. How don't we listen? We don't listen in three central modes: focusing on ourselves, reacting out of our own feelings, and presuming that we have heard. Let's have a further look at these behaviors.

Self-Focus Interferes With Listening

To listen means to focus on the speaker and on the message *he* or *she* is trying to convey. This information isn't necessarily factual; it could be about the speaker's feelings or needs. When you don't listen effectively, that focus switches. The one who is *supposed to listen* focuses instead on his or her own agenda. In the following interaction, Mandy doesn't hear John because she is focused on herself.

John: I hate my job, I just hate the bickering and sniping that goes on there.

Mandy: I am so glad that I left that place. I think you should have left long ago.

Mandy's advice might be right, but she is not focusing on John. She is not attentive to what John is feeling. She's not taking the time to listen to the way that bickering and sniping are affecting him. She focuses on *her* feelings and *her* opinion. Mandy might say in her defense, "I know exactly what he is feeling—that's why I left there." But if Mandy understands John, she is not communicating the understanding to him. She is doing something else: she is talking about *herself*. She talks about *her* relief at leaving, *her* advice as to what he should do, and she rebukes him for not having taken the action she deems appropriate.

All bad habits of non-listening share the proclivity to talk about self rather than to listen to the other. For example, Rolando announces, "I'm not going to play in Little League this year." When his dad responds, "Look, I've paid fifty bucks for equipment. There's no way you're not going to play" the dad is talking about *his* expenses and *his* decision. He might be teaching his son about responsible decision making, but he is not listening. He does not try to learn why Rolando does not want to play baseball. In another instance, when Tony happily starts to describe a great meal at a new restaurant and Ted replies, "I ate there when it first opened. I've heard it's already started to go downhill," Ted has turned the focus away from Tony and put it where he likes it to be, on himself. In a similar manner, when Shelly complained to her husband, Adam, "I felt foolish at your company's dinner when you left me for half an hour while you talked to your boss," Adam's defense focuses on Adam. He acts out of *his* vulnerability and *his* concerns when he says, "What am I supposed to do? He pays my salary. He wanted to talk. I had no choice!" He doesn't try to learn anything about his wife's discomfort, awkwardness, hurt, embarrassment, fear, or shyness.

Bobbie, a pert thirty-seven-year-old woman, described the effect that being heard had on her and on her feelings of closeness with her husband.

I have been trying to tell Brent for at least two years that I am just too lonely. I wanted him to travel less. Every time I tried to talk about it he would say, "You have to find more friends" or "How successful would I be as a head hunter if I couldn't travel?" Then last week, I told him again that it isn't that I need more friends. I have plenty, but I just miss him. I want to be with him. I don't know if I said it differently or if he was finally ready to hear me, but he listened and really got it. He finally heard what it's been like for me to be lonely for him, to want to be with him, to do sports together or to have dinner with friends. At least, I know he knows how I've been feeling. We haven't been this close in years.

When we seem to listen but focus instead on ourselves, we give *our* views, *our* feelings, *our* advice, *our* opinions, *our* experience. In this way, we inevitably fail to hear and understand the speaker. Ironically, we assume that this speaker, whom we haven't really heard or understood, will now listen to what we are saying. It's no wonder that the failure to listen results in such sad lack of contact!

Listener's Own Feelings Interfere With Listening

When someone is talking to you, are you aware of your own feelings? Do you even know that you are having feelings? Feelings happening within you generate reactions that can stymie the way you listen to someone else. When you feel hurt or threatened, you will be inclined to defend rather than to listen. For example, Alicia says, "You pay more attention to your parents than you do to me." Her husband Charlie's response was to defend himself, and his answer is fueled by hurt or resentment at Alicia's accusation. "I barely see them. For Pete's sake, they're in their eighties! They need a lot more attention from me than I give them."

Charlie's justification of his behavior toward his parents and his hurt feelings distract him from listening to Alicia's loneliness or insecurity. In another interaction, Jill, a teenager, is fearful that her parents are going to limit her freedom. Her father says, "You have just one more week to be looking for a summer job. You better get your priorities right. You're spending too much time at the mall." Jill doesn't listen to him because her fear molds her reactions. The best defense is a good offense. "You don't trust me. You never have," she tells her dad angrily. "You'd never talk that way to Joe. He can do no wrong." This teenager hasn't heard her father's worry or his concern that she have a productive summer. She hears his warning about potential limits to her freedom and fun. Feeling fear or panic, she verbally attacks her father.

Joanna, a mother of two tots, tells her sister Louise that she is thinking of separating from her husband of seven years. Louise is filled with concern for her sister and for her two nieces. Louise doesn't listen to her sister's loneliness and frustration. Full of fear, she advises, "Don't think the single life is so great. Maybe Mark isn't perfect, but you've got to give him time to grow up." Fear provokes advice and warnings from Louise. Her reaction trumps the attentive listening that Joanna needs and which Louise could provide if she held her own feelings in check.

It is ironic that the one listening is often not able to hear the speaker's message, information, or feelings because he or she is not listening well enough to his or her own feelings. Those personal feelings get in the way of listening to someone else's feelings.

Presumption Interferes With Listening

Even if you have succeeded in focusing on the speaker, you may, nonetheless, undermine your efforts to listen by making presumptions. *We all tend to make two assumptions: First, we presume that we know what the speaker really means; second, we presume that the speaker knows that we understand.* Each assumption excuses us from confirming with the speaker that what we are hearing is what he or she is trying to say.

Jonathan (husband): We are really not in good shape financially this month.

Terry (wife): Don't start. I haven't bought a thing for myself. The only money I've spent has been on groceries and on the kids' new sneakers.

Terry presumes that her husband is criticizing her for excessive spending. She doesn't stop to hear his anxiety about covering the bills. He might be having many worries about his job or his earning power. Terry hears none of his feelings. She presumes that he is talking about her and quickly defends.

Dorothy starts to tell her husband, "My mother called about my niece's wedding. I couldn't stop her from telling me what I ought to do about the shower." Her husband, Walter, reacts, "What happened to the plan that you'd get off the phone with her after five minutes? If you allow her to interfere, you'll always be upset. How often do you need to learn that?" Walter presumes that his wife has ignored or forgotten to follow an agreed upon strategy. He proceeds to reprimand her. Dorothy is already feeling defeated in her attempts to limit the way her mother interferes with her plans. Now, she will feel even more discouraged by her husband Walter who has failed to hear and understand her. She needed Walter to hear that she hasn't abandoned her strategy. She is just feeling futility in trying to enforce it.

Assumptions can be costly. Every day, doctors make mistakes by presuming that they have heard a patient without verifying what they have heard. A renowned New York surgeon operated on the left foot of a diabetic patient when it should have been the right one. He was distraught when he told us, "I always check my notes and the case records. This time, I just assumed that I remembered. I would have bet on it." In hospitals, errors based on assumptions cost millions of dollars each year in malpractice suits. They cost even more in the tragic impact they have on the lives of patients and physicians.

Unconfirmed, unchecked assumptions carry a similar cost for businesses. An executive at a national retailer complained, "My buyer assumed that I liked a particular line of suits. On that basis, she made major purchases. I'd said that they were new and interesting, but that's all I said. I can fire her, but we've still got a ton of merchandise that we'll be stuck with."

Assuming that we have heard and understood can conveniently absolve us of the embarrassing chore of confirming the message that we heard. It is tempting to avoid "checking" what we have heard. We want to be viewed as alert, sharp, plugged in. We don't want to be met with sarcastic replies such as, "Evidently that's what I said . . ." or "How many times do I need to repeat it?" So, rather than taking the time and trouble to confirm a message, we risk the assumption that we've got it. Sometimes, we—and others—pay dearly for our assumption.

Presumptions that we understand a message can produce knee-jerk reactions. The one presuming doesn't take time to listen, especially to the feelings of the speaker. If you are the listener, and you are convinced that you know what the speaker is trying to say, you may feel no need to "check out" the accuracy of your assumption. The presumption of understanding hinders the satisfying connection that patient listening can facilitate. Even if the listener actually does fully understand what the speaker is saying, failure to express that understanding can cause frustration and separation. The "listener" in this case presumes that the speaker trusts that he or she is being heard. Typically, people tell themselves: "I don't have to demonstrate understanding or show that I heard this message; she knows I understand."

"*She knows* I understand." That kind of remark is often followed by an irritated spouse or sibling disagreeing, "*I don't know* that you understand! You don't act like you understand. Why don't you show it?" Thus, even if the listener does understand, that doesn't mean that the one speaking experiences understanding.

Listening demands that this presumption (this person will know that I understand what's being said) is also discarded and the effort to communicate empathy is made. Presumptions tend to reveal arrogance in the one assuming. Communicating understanding and really listening calls for some humility.

Communicating understanding and really listening calls for some humility.

Admitting to non-listening behaviors takes humility for all of us. You might like to think that you listen well as a spouse, friend, boss, or parent when you are at home and at work. You are probably not even aware of how frequently you don't listen. Most of us know that our bosses don't listen very well to us. We are sorely aware that our spouses, friends, or children don't pay attention to us either. But, we can be blind to our own poor listening. When we are giving advice and telling people what they should or should not do, we're not aware that we are not listening. When we are responding with our own stories, we don't realize that we're listening to ourselves and not to our friends. When we jump to our defense, we fail to realize that while we are justifying ourselves, we have stopped listening. Before we can learn to listen, we must first identify and heighten our awareness of all the ways that we do not listen.

The next chapters in this section of the book will discuss, in greater depth and detail, some of these common non-listening behaviors. Remember, these behaviors are not "bad" or "unethical." You don't need a lengthy set of listening rules that forbid certain behaviors. Non-listening behaviors are ways of speaking and acting that can readily undermine individuals and groups from really meeting one another, from connecting in mutually satisfying ways. *When we are heard, we feel a sense of relief and a unity with the person listening.* When we endure non-listening treatment from others, we have feelings that are just the opposite. We suffer frustration, loneliness, and disconnection from those with whom we eagerly and even desperately want to be united.

Reflection Questions

@ What behaviors or mannerisms do you exhibit when you're not listening to someone else?

@ Can you recognize non-listening behaviors (identifying, advising, defending, judging) in others who seem to be listening to you? How do these behaviors make you feel?

@ How do you interpret the statement: "listening calls for humility"?

CHAPTER EIGHT

Defending

Think back to the last time that you felt defensive or defended yourself. It felt pretty dissatisfying, didn't it? There's probably no behavior that gets in the way of listening more than defensiveness. Defensiveness prevents real connections between individuals, often between those who most need one another's respect and affection. Verbal self-defense is almost always counterproductive. First, it doesn't really even protect the one who is defending. He or she is already hurt, stung, "gotten," or he or she wouldn't be defending. Second, it leaves the one who spoke feeling frustrated, hurt, or resentful at not being understood. And finally, it is a non-listening behavior. It frequently leads to futile arguments that, in turn, result in further troubling feelings.

Michael's spouse says, "I'm so frustrated that you spend so little time with the children. They need you." Michael reacts in knee-jerk defense of himself, "What are you talking about? I coach Derek's soccer team and I drive Pearl to dance class. I can't please you." Michael hasn't really listened to his wife. Maybe she's concerned that she can't control their oldest boy on her own. Or, she's feeling that Michael isn't home much on the weekends, or perhaps that he is drifting away from the family.

Whatever she is meaning or feeling, Michael hears only something critical about himself. He feels threatened or guilty or hurt or resentful, and reacts without listening. He hears that he is bad, but proclaims that he is good. He hears that his wife doesn't think that he's an attentive father. What he has heard is criticism! What Michael does in reaction is to defend himself. What he hasn't done is to listen to his wife.

What Is Defensiveness?

Defensiveness is a self-protective behavior. Its focus is on "me," and how I can keep out of harm's way. The defensive person sniffs out danger to his or her reputation, ego, or well-being and leaps to ward off "the enemy" with self-justifying comments. The one who is defending himself is not listening to what the speaker is feeling (hurt, anger, fear, loneliness) or what the speaker needs (attention, warmth, support). The message about himself is that he is bad or deficient in some way, and reacts accordingly. For example,

> **Marie complains**: We never seem to have the money to make this house look better.

> **Greg hears**: You are a poor provider. You should ask for a raise. You should get a new job.

> **Greg defends**: You are so spoiled, it's ridiculous! Why don't you make more money instead of making me feel guilty?

If Greg could hear the feelings or message beneath Marie's words, he would hear that she feels inferior to her sister who has just moved into a new house. Marie may fear that her house is starting to look like the unkempt home that she grew up in. If Greg heard her vulnerability and fear, he might show care and sympathy. Instead, he hears only criticisms about himself and reacts in his own defense.

Defensiveness has its roots in hearing a negative message about one's self. The defensive person does not take the time to listen more deeply into what might be happening within the speaker. The defender hears something critical or blaming, and reacts in a self-justifying manner. Without pausing and resisting the temptation to defensiveness, the listen completely misses what the spouse, friend, child, or boss is feeling and

Defensiveness signals that listening to the speaker has ceased.

needing. Defensiveness signals that listening to the speaker has ceased. The defender feels under attack and is at work protecting himself. No understanding of the speaker is gained. There is no mutual appreciation for what each is experiencing. Defensiveness strains any relationship.

None of the above is meant to suggest that the speaker is *never* voicing criticism. In the examples cited, Michael's wife is criticizing him for not spending more time with the children. Maybe Marie is at least implying that Greg is not bringing home enough money. But when Michael and Greg defend themselves, they hear *only* criticism directed their way. They stop connecting and listening for the feelings, needs, thoughts, and perceptions of their wives which prompted those comments—critical or not. Michael and Greg didn't really listen in a way that helped them to understand their wives. They didn't listen beyond the words of criticism for the message that their wives were trying to share. They didn't confirm what they thought they were hearing. Instead, they heard only "attacks" on themselves and their actions, and they defended themselves.

Why Do We Defend?

We are all vulnerable. We need to be liked, respected, and appreciated. We need to feel safe, secure, and valued. The less secure we feel, the more prone we are to sense a personal threat and are thus more ready to defend ourselves.

A sensible mother does not ask a five-year-old sitting on a kitchen floor covered in spilled flour, "Did you get into the flour and make a mess up on the counter again?" She would only be inviting a defensive lie from the frightened child. "No, it wasn't me, Mommy."

As adults, we can feel as vulnerable as the child does; we react just as defensively. An executive at a TV network confessed to us how stupid he feels when he gets defensive at work.

I would like to hear the remarks my boss makes without getting defensive. We had a meeting this week, and as soon as he began to outline some suggestions to improve programming, I couldn't stop myself from coming back with reasons—really excuses—why we hadn't done better. I could see him holding back his annoyance, but I couldn't stop myself.

A potent mechanism is at work here. Even though the executive has the self-awareness to recognize his own defensive tendency, under the pressure of feeling insecure, he can not control his self-justifying and self-defeating behavior.

We can be so insecure that we cannot hear suggestions or constructive criticism. We hear blame or attack, and then defend ourselves. Insecurity hampers our ability to listen to a boss or to an employee. We can feel threatened by a friend commenting on our car or on our golf swing. But we are most vulnerable to being hurt in our closest relationships. While our spouses or partners may be able to be our best friends and supports, they can also be our "intimate enemies," the ones who can wound us most deeply, the ones against whom we must be on guard. This couple demonstrates the pattern:

> **Husband**: I want us to spend more time together. I'm afraid that we could become one of those couples who look at each other like strangers when our last child goes to school.
>
> **Wife hears**: You aren't a good partner. You're avoiding me. If you don't change, I'm going to leave you when our son goes to college.
>
> **Wife defends**: I never have any private time as it is. What more do you want from me? Don't threaten me. It makes me want to spend even less time with you.

It is often difficult to listen purely to your spouse, to hear what he or she is saying about personal needs, feelings, thoughts and wishes. We all tend to hear *about ourselves*— what is said *about us*, and particularly what is being said critically about us. So we react in self-defense.

Defending by Denial

We defend ourselves in many ways. Like the child on the kitchen floor saying, "No, it wasn't me, Mommy," we, too, simply deny responsibility. April had gone with her husband Will to his parents' wedding anniversary. On the way home she complained.

April: You spent the whole time with your brothers and left me sitting with your folks and your sister. You know I don't get along with her, and I never know what to say to your parents.

Will: I did not. They asked me about their taxes. It took twenty minutes.

April: You also deliberately sat as far away from me as possible.

Will: I did not. Jeanne asked me to sit next to her. That's all.

In accusing language, April is trying to tell Will about the sad, lonely, and awkward feelings she had at the dinner. She is also telling him how hurt or resentful she felt by what she perceived as his rejection and insensitivity. Will doesn't even try to hear her. He hears accusation and denies the charges. April felt a sad lack of rapport with Will throughout the evening; she probably felt more alone after trying to talk about it.

Defending by Disputing Perceptions

Many interactions become futile arguments that boil down to whose perception is right. When what we are hearing about our behavior and ourselves is threatening, we ignore the speaker's feelings. We rebut the threat. April's words imply many feelings, especially hurt. Will dismisses her feelings by denying the accuracy of her perception, "I didn't leave you—I was talking with my brothers." "I didn't choose not to sit with you—I accepted Jeanne's invitation to sit with her." We go on the defensive because we don't like or don't agree with the description or perception of our actions. But the speaker deserves to have his or her emotions heard. Will believes that April's perception that he actively abandoned her is inaccurate, but her perception has caused her great distress. If he could refrain from arguing about her perception, he might understand her feelings and react with compassion. Whether or not she is "right," she still spent a lonely and hurt-filled evening. Her loneliness and hurt cannot be disputed. When we deny the validity of the speaker's remark, we abruptly stop the speaker in order to defend ourselves. We don't, however, stop ourselves from a knee-jerk defense of ourselves. And we don't take the time to listen for the feelings that underlie the speaker's accusation.

When Hank is frustrated because he thinks Jay didn't return a borrowed tool, Jay's denial leaves Hank alone in his frustration. He is still missing his tool whether or not Jay has it. When a mother is hurt because she thinks her son has forgotten her birthday, her sadness deserves to be heard and understood. Her son's denial doesn't help. "That's not true," he insists. "I was thinking of you. I just got tied up at work." His reaction doesn't communicate understanding to her. It merely rejects her interpretation of his failure to call. Rejecting another's critical perception of us is an effort that focuses on defending ourselves, not allowing ourselves to be seen as bad or at fault.

Establishing the "rightness" or "wrongness" of perceptions wastes time. It could be spent trying to understand. When the argument pertains to events or perceptions of events that occurred in the past, the battle becomes a test of whose memory is more exact. The battle is lightheartedly portrayed by characters in the musical *Gigi* in the song "I Remember It Well."

We met at 9

We met at 8

I was on time

No, you were late

Ah yes, I remember it well

We dined with friends

We dined alone

A tenor sang

A baritone

Ah yes, I remember it well.

The test of memories in real life is frequently not at all lighthearted. For William and Leah, the dispute is quite hurtful.

William: Remember the night I called you from London about closing the biggest deal of my life, you would not stop talking about how the damn toilet kept overflowing.

Leah: That is just not true. I remember clearly congratulating you and asking where you and your team were going to celebrate.

It is futile for both of them to argue over the truth of an event that happened years ago. William's feelings of hurt and resentment, still sharp, are not addressed at all. Instead, the focus becomes a futile and distracting effort to establish "the truth" about that call. Daniel L. Schacter, a professor at Harvard and author of *The Seven Sins of Memory: How the Mind Forgets and Remembers*, writes, "Research also reveals an egocentric bias, meaning we remember the part of the event in ways that reflect positively our current self."

Feelings that demand to be aired and heard are lost frequently in interactions that become hotly contested debates that center on our own need to be right.

Defending by Counterattacking

Adhering to the maxim that the best defense is a good offense, we often attack the speaker when we feel most defensive. Instead of denying or refuting the accusation that we have heard, we go directly after the speaker and attack. Rebecca reprimands her brother David:

Rebecca: I'm worried that you are not working hard at your job. I'm afraid that if you don't change, you will be out of work again.

David: Who are you to tell me? You've never had to go look for a job. You get easy jobs and then spend your time on the phone. You are lazy!

David doesn't listen to her concern for him; he hears attack and promptly launches a counterattack. In the following example, Stephanie doesn't listen to her father when he expresses impatience with her effort at school.

Father: You are going to seriously regret the way that you have neglected your schoolwork. You will have no chance of getting into a good college.

Instead of listening, she defends by hitting him where he is vulnerable.

Stephanie: How do you know? It's not like you went to college. So don't tell me.

Stephanie could have heard her father's love for her, could have heard his desire that she succeed, could have heard his fear that she will share the handicaps that his lack of education has caused him. Instead, she hears blame and decides to belittle him in her own defense. The person who is counterattacking refuses to listen beyond criticism, blame, or attack and reacts instead by targeting the "attacker." No meeting or exchange results from the defensive attack. The perceived enemy is driven back. Both speaker and defender are left frustrated and hurt.

Defending by Instilling Guilt

Defending by attacking the speaker sometimes takes on a less flagrant character than an outright verbal assault. In this type of interchange, we might defend ourselves by attempting to make the speaker feel guilty. The hope of this defense is that the one accusing us will feel remorse and withdraw the charge. In utter frustration, Carlos shouts at his friend Tony.

Carlos: What is wrong with you? You were supposed to pick me up three hours ago. I've wasted a whole morning.

Tony defends himself by revealing his hurt and pointing to the injustice of Carlos' remark.

Tony: Hey man, that really hurts. I'd never keep you waiting on purpose. You know that. I had some heavy duty stuff with my dad. You know how sick he's been.

Tony's words contain the message: "How can you be so unfair when I'm such a good friend and such a good son? You should apologize for your attack and your words and renew your care and respect for me."

In another example of guilt-inducing defense, a father reprimands his son Harry, a lawyer, for failing to review the living will that he and his wife had prepared. Harry could not listen to his father's disappointment or concern that if anything happened to him or to his wife, it could leave them without the will's protection. Instead, Harry feels like a kid being blamed for irresponsibility. He's particularly vulnerable to blame since he really did forget about the will. Instead of listening to and responding to his father's feelings, Harry defends himself.

> **Harry**: God, Dad. I'm sorry. But you know the pressure I'm under. All hell is breaking loose on the construction site, and I'm being asked to take over more and more responsibility. You know, the kids have been sick this week. I haven't felt well myself, but I can't take any time off.

The message in Harry's words is: "Dad, stop being selfish. I am absolutely overwhelmed. Feel some compassion for me. In fact, you should feel guilty for adding to my burden."

The son's self-serving defense might cover his failure; it most assuredly keeps him from hearing an aging parent's concern and worry. Defending by attempting to instill guilt can also foster distrust. The dad might retreat, but he might also have to struggle now with trusting his son. Carlos might stop shouting at Tony, but he might also start questioning how truthful Tony is. Defensiveness exacts a toll on all relationships.

Defensiveness exacts a toll on all relationships.

Reflection Questions

@ Think of an occasion when you acted defensively toward another person. Now recall a time when you were able to put defensiveness aside, and get into the speaker's shoes.

@ Do you know what factors or circumstances trigger defensiveness in you?

@ Do you recall one or more occasions when you defended yourself by trying to make another person feel guilty?

CHAPTER NINE

Identifying the "Me Too" Syndrome

No form of non-listening behavior more blatantly shifts the focus of attention away from the speaker than the "me too" syndrome. It works like this: As you listen to someone, you're reminded of your own experiences and you respond with a "me too" response.

Harriet starts to tell her friend Laurie, "I got an unbelievable deal on my new car, and they even tossed in a bunch of extras like a sun roof and CD player." Laurie is quick to counter, "You won't believe this, but I did too. They gave me a great trade-in and then knocked down the price. Then, they gave me incredible financing." It's hard to know what Laurie's motivation was. What she heard from Harriet, however, triggered a "me too" response that shifted the focus from her friend to herself. Harriet's story became a springboard for telling her own. Perhaps she felt envy and wanted to top Harriet. Maybe she wanted "the floor." She may have wished to simply "join in" the good news. Whatever her intent, she talked about herself instead of listening to her friend.

Need for Attention

We all want to be noticed and acknowledged. We like it when people listen to us. These desires can get in the way of giving that attention even to those we love. A close friend says, "I had a terrible night's sleep." You reply, "I haven't slept well for weeks, ever since I began taking that blood pressure medication." Your brother complains, "Man, I have lost a bundle lately in the market." You reply, "You have! I am down thirty percent since January. I got into some tech stocks that my broker thought were a good deal. They turned out to be a disaster. I tell you, I did better before I had a broker."

In one sense there is potential for good within these exchanges. There is a momentary experience of empathy. The speaker thinks: "You must know what I mean if you came up with a comparable experience so quickly!" At times, there is even the comfort of commiseration. "Misery loves company." If the person speaking needs, however, to be heard, thoroughly and deeply, the quick "me too" is discouraging. It usually signals that the listener is about to grab the focus. The original speaker is then in the uncomfortable spot of having to demand attention once again.

Two high school seniors face the "me too" dilemma when they meet on their way to school. One says, "I'm so excited. I just got accepted to my first choice for college!" The second one says, "Me too!" Both are excited. Both have a story to tell in their quest to get into college. The exchange—a synergy of excitement—may meet their need in interacting. But if the first senior feared that she might not get into any college and is now surprised to find herself going to her preferred school, she may want to talk a great deal more. Ideally, her friend will have the sensitivity to withhold further expressions of her own excitement in order to listen. If she doesn't put her ebullience aside temporarily, her friend is faced with an awkward choice. She could give up talking about her fears and her surprise. Or, she could demand that her friend suspend her excitement and listen.

It is natural for many of us to talk about ourselves and to meet our need for attention. So often when someone speaks, we are reminded of ourselves and we grab the spotlight. We usually don't intend to avoid listening, but our need for recognition forms a habit of "me too" interruptions. Our friend, parent, or colleague says something that reminds us about some personal experience of our own and we're off and running. In short, we become the focus of the interaction.

Need to Win or At Least Not to Lose

Sometimes in our fear of seeming to be "second best," we find it very difficult to listen. Someone else's event or good fortune could make them seem more fortunate or successful than we are. So, we jump in with our own claim to fame. Jacob recounts an event from his vacation. "We were in this beautiful hotel at Disney World when who walks into the lobby but Jane Seymour. Later, we nearly fainted when we ended up sitting at a table next to hers in the restaurant." The story is a bit threatening to Jacob's sister. So, she counters with her own adventure. "I had the same thing happen in New York. Chad and I were staying at the Plaza, and right next to us at registration was Tom Hanks and his wife. When we were waiting for a table in the

Oak Room, the maitre d' said, 'You're in luck. I'm seating you at the table next to Tom Hanks and his party.' We could hear their whole conversation."

If someone has been on a cruise, we've been on a better ocean liner. If a friend has been to a NASCAR race, we've been to the Indy 500. If a colleague caught a large fish, we caught a larger one. We try not to be too obvious in our "Can you top this?" rejoinder. But, we can't keep quiet and listen appreciatively. We feel diminished by someone's account of good fortune, and we feel the need to surpass or at least match it.

A young woman told us what family get-togethers are like for her.

It's like a contest when we get together. I don't even try to talk about anything meaningful that has happened to me. Everyone has to top the person who is talking. It doesn't matter what the topic is. I say very little. Dinnertimes are the worst. Yet, they are forever saying, "We've all got to get together for the holidays." It's sad.

Competitive "me too" responses can become the "modus operandi" of family conversations, replacing thoughtful exchanges. The pattern can become such a familiar form of interaction that some members of the family fail to recognize how hurtful it is to others. It's no surprise that a similar type of competitive interchange may occur in business, creating a work environment that discourages open, trusting dialogue.

Identifying as an Attempt to Empathize

Identifying with the speaker by saying "me too" is a knee-jerk reaction that allows us to talk about ourselves either by force of habit or as a way to avoid feeling inferior. But sometimes it represents a conscious effort to empathize with the one speaking. Saying "me too" can be a way of trying to say, "I've been there myself. Therefore, I understand." For example, Benny, an eight-year-old, says,

"My teacher doesn't like me. She thinks I'm not trying." Benny's dad tries to comfort by showing he had the same feeling as a child. "I know just how you feel. You know when I was in your grade, I had a teacher just like yours. She never liked me, but I didn't let her get to me."

Benny's dad means well. He wants to make his son feel better and hopes that his story will do the trick. It might. The danger, though, is that Dad might have to start inventing identifying experiences to show Benny that he understands. Identification has limits as a way to communicate understanding. It can also strain trust. Did you really have that experience or are you just saying so to make me feel better?

Identification also presumes that what the listener has experienced is identical to what the speaker is expressing. Since each person is unique, the presumption is, well, rather presumptuous. A sixth-grade teacher remarked, "I hate it when someone says, 'I know just how you feel.' Last week another teacher said to me, 'I had a smart kid who wouldn't work and whose parents wouldn't believe me. It was just like the one you are talking about.' I know she was trying to make me feel better, but she doesn't know how I feel. How could she? I haven't even gotten clear what I feel."

In the following example, a friend feels the frustration of not being heard and being told, in essence, that she's not unique.

Samantha: I dread getting old. It seems like every other day I get a new reminder that aging is a pain, literally.

Blythe: Oh, me too. I know exactly what you mean. I thought dealing with gray hair was bad, but I learned that I can at least dye my hair. But yesterday, I saw some wrinkles around my eyes that look permanent.

Blythe may be trying to make her friend feel better by demonstrating that they are in this "aging misery" together.

But Blythe looks unusually young for her age, and if she has wrinkles around her eyes, they are not visible to Samantha. So Blythe's "me too" comes across as patronizing, prompting Samantha to say, "What are you talking about? Your face is as smooth as when you were thirty." If they're not careful, they could end up arguing—a sad result when Samantha's original need in sharing was to be heard in her discouragement. Making Samantha feel better might have been more effectively accomplished if Blythe had taken time to hear the uniqueness of Samantha's experience.

Each of us is unique. We are a certain age, from specific parents, from a definite locale. We are of a particular race , of a particular nationality and temperament, educated in particular schools, raised in a certain religion. With all these differences, it is unreasonable for someone to presume to have had precisely the same feelings that we are describing. How false it really is to say, "I know just how you feel," or, "I had the same feeling," or, "The same thing happened to me"? The truth may be that a friend or family member, boss or colleague could have had a feeling that seems similar. That possibility, however, does not permit the person to presume understanding. Such presumption of understanding strips away the uniqueness of the speaker, however good the "listener's" intention. In both ways, presuming and shifting the focus, this "me too" empathy is a poor way of listening. Later in the book we will demonstrate how the listener can draw from experiences that seem similar to the speaker's to communicate empathy, but without the presumption of identification.

Identifying as an Effort to Comfort, Encourage, or Motivate

Empathy is strained when the one who could be listening chooses to identify with the speaker for purposes other than to communicate understanding. When Benny's dad identified with his eight-year-old's problem with his teacher, he had another agenda than trying to convey to his son that he fully understood his son's sadness. He wanted to comfort his son as well as to advise him to triumph over his feelings of hurt just as his dad had done. Encouragement and advice try to achieve different goals than listening, even when they are disguised as empathy. Comforting his son and teaching him to cope with difficult feelings are admirable, fatherly behaviors. They definitely have their place in child-rearing. But it is important for dads and moms, and for anyone wanting to learn to listen, that they distinguish these behaviors from focused listening. Troy, a sophomore in college, talks to an older friend.

> **Troy**: I've about had it with school. I'm always behind and am bored stiff in my classes. I could work in my dad's construction company and make some serious money.

> **Simon**: I went through the same feelings in my sophomore year at Duke. I could have cared less, but I stuck it out and then junior and senior years were pretty good. I actually ended up graduating cum laude. Hang in there, Dude. It's worth it.

Simon's agenda is to boast as well as to encourage Troy to stay in school. He says that he had the same feelings as Troy but shows no real understanding. He doesn't listen to Troy, doesn't attempt to learn what Troy is actually feeling about himself, about school, or about earning money. He says, "me too," "been there," but identifies with Troy's feelings only on the most superficial level before getting to his real agenda: talking about his own success and urging Troy to persevere.

Genna, the mother of twins, complained in tears to her older sister.

Genna: I cannot get back to the weight I want. When Tina was born I lost fifteen pounds in like two months. But not this time. I have tried and tried and I'm afraid I'll stay like this.

Susan: I went through the same thing after Eli. I thought I'd never get back in shape. But it goes away, don't worry.

Susan doesn't take time to listen to her sister's feelings of helplessness and fear. In order to comfort and to encourage her sister, she quickly says she has been there. The effect of her words can actually be hurtful. They can be heard by her vulnerable sister as somewhat dismissive of her feelings of futility and discouragement. If Susan really did experience such painful feelings, she is in a unique position to hear how frightening they are for Genna. She could listen with real understanding. Her agenda, instead, is to comfort not by listening which takes time and focus, but by facile identification.

Listening demands that we drop any other agenda, clearing the way for us simply to make the effort to understand the speaker. It is very difficult "just" to listen. Our own story, and agendas of helping, motivating, and comforting, keep getting in the way.

Reflection Questions

....

@ Under what circumstances are you more likely to respond with "me too . . ." stories instead of listening? Do you react this way with a particular person or persons?

@ Can you name those who offer "me too . . . " responses when you need them to listen to you?

@ Describe the differences between identification that contributes to empathy, and identification that only leads the would-be listener to more self-centered attention and talk.

CHAPTER TEN

Giving
Advice

We don't listen because we are intent on doing something else: distractedly watching TV or reading the paper, thinking of what we are going to say when the speaker stops talking, defending ourselves from perceived attack. At times we don't listen because as born storytellers we enjoy telling our own story. We also don't listen because we are born helpers. One rainy afternoon, we, the authors, were crossing a street in mid-town Manhattan when a young woman tripped at the curb, fell, and dropped her papers, cell phone, and water bottle. Immediately, three or four men and women moved quickly to make sure she was not hurt while others gathered her belongings. Supposedly cold, indifferent New Yorkers rushed to help a stranger. Despite images of callous city dwellers, they reached out to offer aid. They are typical of most of us. We react to accidents and all kinds of perceived need with assistance.

Similarly in conversation, we react in a helpful manner when we hear that the person speaking is in some difficulty or has a problem or is confused. We want to help with suggestions and solutions. Simply listening with full attention to the feelings, needs, and thoughts of the person talking is usually not considered an option, and if it were considered, it probably would be deemed insufficient. We feel compelled to help—not by giving empathy, but by offering advice. Our offer of "helpful" advice is based on a whole list of assumptions.

- I have understood your difficulty.
- I have answers to your problem.
- You want my solutions.
- You haven't thought of these solutions yourself.
- You are able to execute the solutions that I propose.

These presumptions are rarely confirmed by "checking them out" with the speaker.

We hear a problem, possibly ask a few questions to clarify, and then begin advising and suggesting. We don't relate back to the speaker what we are hearing to confirm that we have truly understood. We don't ask if the speaker wants our advice. We don't think to find out if the speaker has already considered the solutions that we are offering, and we don't determine whether the person is able to do what we are suggesting. We presume and forge ahead with our advice and opinion. For example, Claudia, a sales representative for a computer firm who lives in Chicago, is talking to her Aunt Jane:

Claudia: I'm so fed up with the creeps that I've been dating. I don't know if there are any decent men out there. Sometimes I think something must be wrong with me. My friends are all getting married.

Aunt Jane: You work too hard. You'll never meet anyone unless you make yourself more available.

Aunt Jane presumes that she has heard her niece's problem: lack of dates due to overwork at the expense of an active social life. She presumes that she has it right and that Claudia wants and needs her advice. She doesn't confirm any of this with her niece. Aunt Jane is there to solve her niece's problem. She doesn't listen to Claudia's discouragement and self-doubt, doesn't invite Claudia to talk about her frustrating dating experiences, and doesn't communicate to Claudia that she understands. She is not focused on trying to understand; she is busy doing something else: providing a solution to a problem.

A similar kind of interaction occurs in another setting. Charlie, an ambitious owner of a small company, is sitting in a clinic's examining room and talking to his doctor.

> **Charlie**: I've been feeling terribly tired. I'm not sleeping that well, waking up in the night and not getting back to sleep. I also think my memory's slipping.

> **Doctor**: You can't keep working the hours you do without paying a price. Your cognitive skills are affected by lack of sleep. I'll write you a prescription for a mild sleeping pill, but slow down and take more time off. Get out on your boat more.

The doctor presumes that he knows the problem: too much work, too little play. And he has the answer: a gentle sleeping aid and more rest and exercise. In this particular case, he did not listen long enough to hear Charlie trying to admit to a drug problem that his wife had begged him to discuss with the doctor. Charlie's first remarks were a hesitant introduction. When the doctor quickly reacted with diagnosis and remedy, Charlie was relieved, yet also disappointed that he did not have to admit to a deeper problem. The doctor doesn't ask Charlie about his work habits. He presumes overwork on the basis of past perceptions that he has had of his patient. He doesn't take the time to listen to Charlie's own views of his disturbed sleep patterns, his fatigue, or his memory lapses. He spends no time really listening. He doesn't have to. He knows the problem and provides the solution. "Next."

Presuming that our suggested solutions are ones that the speaker has not considered would appear to be a rather arrogant presumption. What makes us so creative and wise that we can, on a moment's notice, provide answers to this person's life that he or she has failed to realize? When we, the authors, were researching our book *Sick and Tired of Feeling Sick and Tired: Living With Invisible Chronic Illness*, we heard repeatedly from individuals a similar frustration with advice. A woman with multiple sclerosis spoke for many with illness when she told us,

> I am so fed up with people, even my family, telling me what to do to feel better: get more exercise, rest more, have a more positive attitude, pray more, try this diet, try this doctor. They don't ask if I pray or exercise or anything. I've had MS for nine years. Don't they think I would know more about my illness, let alone about myself, than they do? I know they mean well, but I hate the advice.

A woman who had been pregnant with twins only to lose one and then the other in miscarriage told us,

> I don't leave the house. I'm too afraid that I'll meet someone who will offer stupid clichés that are supposed to make me feel better. "You'll have other children." Or, "Just trust in God." I can't stand to hear that stuff anymore. I'm afraid I'll lash out at them. I'm better off avoiding people.

It would probably be too painful for these advice givers to listen deeply to the grieving woman's intense sorrow and anger and hopelessness. Listening would demand much. Advice costs little and is often worth less.

The presumption that advice offered can be implemented by the one receiving it can have unwitting, even harmful, consequences. An elderly man who lost his wife in an auto accident was hospitalized with severe depression. He was finally released into our care and began to try to get his life together. The depression, however, clung to him like a black, leaden cloak. Each day he struggled to find meaning in any activity. Each day demanded enormous courage to resist despair and to carry out the simplest responsibilities. One day he arrived for therapy distressed and particularly depressed. After some reflection he admitted,

> I feel like a failure. Two friends, one on Tuesday and another yesterday, gave me pep talks and told me what I ought to be doing—stay in the tennis group, play with the seniors in Thursday golf, and some other things they say I should do. I felt much worse afterward. They don't understand. I can't do it.

The friends meant well. The widower knew that. But instead of communicating respectful understanding, in their concern and worry, they thought that they must motivate him to action. They advised activities, however, beyond his present ability. Their presumption that their suggestions would be beneficial revealed their disconnect from his condition. Consequently he felt lonelier, more inadequate, and more depressed. People who make presumptions can miss the speaker's reality and, in doing so, offer advice that is not only irrelevant and annoying but even harmful.

Effects of Advice-Giving: Dependency

Advice can engender non-healthy results even when it seems helpful. A parent who always has the solution for his child's problems can rear a son or a daughter who is insecure and fearful. A wise parent knows when to listen or at least to be quiet so that the child can develop confidence in his or her ability to make decisions. A manager is effective not if he resolves every issue, but if, by listening, he allows employees to discover their own competence. The old maxim seems wise and apt, "Give a man a fish and he eats for a day; teach a man to fish and he eats for a lifetime."

A senior executive at a Wall Street corporation complained about one of his managers.

He micromanages all of his people. They are afraid to try anything on their own. They need his approval on the smallest decisions. I get no new ideas from his group. He was a good producer, but he is a lousy manager.

Psychologists unwittingly can foster dependent clients by conditioning them to rely on the therapist for each of life's decisions. The goal of therapy—to free individuals to trust themselves and to be confident that they can cope with the challenges that they face in life—is defeated. A grateful mother of four children aged six to seventeen spoke to us of her counselor.

I had a therapist that let me call her day or night. I'd call her whenever I felt down or had a problem. She knew how to make me feel better and had great advice. But she moved. My new therapist is so different. For one thing I can't call unless there's an emergency. But by the time my appointment comes around, I've usually figured out what I've got to do. She won't give me answers. She listens and helps me to figure out what I've got to do. It's amazing. I thought my other counselor was good. But I am doing much better now thanks to this new therapist.

Pharmaceutical companies in their marketing effort to please physicians or protect themselves from litigious consumers undermine patients' self-reliance with the mantra, "Be sure and talk to your doctor." What we really need to hear is, "Know thyself."

Effects of Advice-Giving: Argument

A frequent, ironic consequence of the effort to help by giving advice is an argument. For example, Jerry is out walking with his brother Rick after the family Thanksgiving dinner.

Jerry: Work stinks. I've got a new boss who is out to make my life miserable. She blames me for stuff that has nothing to do with me. Monday she asked me why I hadn't gotten a report done that she had never talked about.

Rick: Sometimes you've got to kill 'em with kindness. Why don't you check her out in her office every morning? Ask her how she's doing. Be real friendly.

Jerry: Are you nuts? I try to avoid her. What a way to start my day talking to her.

Rick: Right. But that could be the problem. She senses your dislike. Let her know you like her.

Jerry: She wouldn't buy it. And I don't like her.

Rick: For God's sake, act like you do. Maybe she's vulnerable. She's new in the job. Be nice to her.

Jerry: You don't get it. Look, let's drop it.

Rick utters a profanity, and they head back to the house not talking.

Rick is trying to help with specific advice, and he wants that advice accepted. When it isn't, he starts to get impatient: "For God's sake, act like you do." Jerry is frustrated at getting advice that he can't picture implementing. "You don't get it." He doesn't experience Rick's understanding, but senses his growing irritation. He regrets that he mentioned his job. Both feel lousy.

Advice often is met by a "yes, but" response that invites more advice followed by more "yes, buts" leading to tension and hurt feelings. Two college women are talking.

Erin: There is this really cute guy in French class that I would love to date. Like, he must have lived in France. He speaks French really well.

Wendy: Why don't you ask him before class where he learned to speak French?

Erin: Yes, but there's no way. He'd think like I'm coming on to him.

Wendy: No he wouldn't. He'd be complimented.

Erin: Maybe. I doubt it.

Wendy: Look, invite him to the party Friday. Tell him there will be a bunch of kids from all over.

Erin: Right, I just walk up to him out of nowhere and ask him. He'd think I'm weird.

Wendy: That's why you never go out. You won't even try.

Erin: That's crap. Just forget it.

Wendy moves quickly to give advice, gets immediately hurt when her advice is rejected and then resorts to blaming her friend for not trying. More often than not advice is found unhelpful and rejected. The person offering the advice will usually attempt a few more suggestions then begin to feel impatient or hurt. In the end, the advice-giver may note that an argument has started but may fail to see how giving advice led to it.

Effects of Advice-Giving: Guilt

Advice is intended to help, to relieve the speaker's distress, to solve his or her problem. Sometimes the advice instead produces more distress, leaving the speaker feeling guilty that he or she cannot do what the advice-giver suggests. The widower who could not resume his tennis and golf activities felt more depressed than before receiving the advice. He felt guilty now that he was failing his friends. A divorced father can unintentionally instill guilt in his daughter when advising her to "be nice to your stepmom" while the young girl is filled with torn feelings—loyalty to her mother and anger toward this "new woman." When she can't "be nice," she feels as though she's a bad daughter. An unemployed forty-year-old who is advised to keep making phone calls to companies in an effort to find work feels guilty knowing he just cannot continue to make these "cold" calls, all the while being aware that one of them just possibly could lead to a job. A woman is told by her doctor that with her family history of diabetes and high blood pressure, she must lose weight. Yet, the woman who wants to be alive to see her daughters grow up can't picture a life of everyday deprivation and restriction. So she says "yes" to the doctor but feels phony and guilty knowing that she will not diet.

It is easy to give advice, to tell someone what to do: leave a husband who is unloving or abusive, leave a job that is unsatisfying, move away from interfering in-laws. It is just as easy to be totally unaware that we can be making the person feel guilt, as though he or she is bad or a failure for not being able to follow our advice.

Other Forms of Helping
That Substitute for Listening

The desire to help with words of encouragement also gets in the way of listening. No sooner has a widow said, "I

The desire to help with words of encouragement also gets in the way of listening. so miss Harold," than a friend responds, "Time heals all wounds." As soon as Jack says, "I just don't know what is going to become of my son," his friend Joe says, "Give him time. He'll be fine." Instead of the widow being heard in her grief or the father listened to in his anxiety, they are offered words of encouragement. The old Western song says, "Seldom is heard a discouraging word." In life, often is heard an encouraging word that rarely provides real comfort.

It is an automatic response for most of us to produce some soothing, pick-me-up words when we hear sadness, fear, or sorrow. We want to help, or we simply can't tolerate pain. In a very real way, we are helpless. We can't bring back a husband who has died. We can't guarantee that a son will mature, just as we can't come up with a pain-free diet or provide a job for an unemployed relative or a girlfriend for our single friend. So we offer words of encouragement or advice. Other than a miracle "cure," what the individual that we are anxious to help really needs is our attentive listening, not our nosegays that are meant to soothe. The mother who has lost the twin babies she was carrying stayed indoors to avoid such "help," such "encouragement." She needed to talk, but only

We want someone to show his or her care, not by presuming to offer help, but by listening.

if she had the space to cry out her pain and to be heard. We all have that need to express our fears, doubts, hurts, and frustrations. We want to be heard and to be understood. There is some mysterious healing that occurs when we can share our burden and have someone listen. We don't want someone else's answers that we then have to acknowledge or fend off. We don't want someone taking a superior position to us and start telling us what to do. We want someone to show his or her care, not by presuming to offer help, but by listening. We want to say, "Please don't tell me what I should or shouldn't do. Just listen. Show me that you understand."

Reflection Questions

- Is listening an adequate response when someone shares information that you view as a serious problem?

- Are there individuals you can listen to without jumping in with advice or correction? If so, why?

- What are your feelings or reactions when someone responds to you with advice instead of simply listening?

CHAPTER ELEVEN

Judging

When we listen we hear beneath common words and expressions to the singular, unique feelings and experience of the individual. Our child can say, as a million other children have said, "Nobody likes me," but he is our particular Bobby with feelings of hurt or loneliness or sadness that are his own. No one has actually felt what Bobby feels. There is only one Bobby. When we listen we meet him in his personal and singular experience. We learn about him, learn to appreciate his specialness and difference. Sean's wife might tell him, "I am terrified to start looking for a job. I feel so inadequate and I feel stupid for feeling that way." She can sound like many women who are reentering the work world after years of child rearing. But she is not "many women," she is Judy—no one else. She has been formed by a million life experiences from childhood, through school, through marriage and mothering. She is literally one of a kind, and when Sean truly listens, he can hear her as she experiences herself. He can discover dimensions of her, nuances that he had not appreciated. Listening connects us with the uniqueness of a person in a way that nourishes both us and the individual heard.

Judging does the opposite. Instead of focusing on the unique individual, we classify the person as being like others. Bobby is judged "immature" like many other slow developers. Judy is seen as "inadequate housewife" as are many women whose lives have been taken up primarily with children and home. When we judge we attempt to know the person by comparing him to others and by categorizing him as part of a group.

Listening connects us with the uniqueness of a person in a way that nourishes both us and the individual heard.

- John is shy—like all quiet and timid people.
- Melissa is energetic—like all other healthy young women.
- Jacque is aggressive—like all other competitive men.
- Pat is arrogant—like all other wealthy executives.

Judging is a natural human activity. Faced with a bewildering amount of data, our intelligence tries to make sense of it all, tries to put some order into all the disparateness, by categorizing into groups. We attempt to simplify all the myriad individual items, things, persons into classifications. Instead of billions of flowers, we group them as roses, tulips, daffodils, or geraniums. The mind needs to sort out reality in this manner. The danger when we do classify human beings is that we can fail to listen to and to appreciate the individual. Twyla, a very efficient administrator, talked of an encounter that demonstrates this point.

> *I had to interview several women for the child-care center. In the afternoon this woman walked in looking like she'd been in a wind tunnel. She had this wild hair and was wearing a long billowy dress. It wasn't very nice of me, but I immediately judged her as a "nuts-berries-granola person." When she spoke she was actually quite articulate, knowledgeable about children, and straightforward. I had to do mental double takes, because I kept expecting her to sound like a spaced out hippie of the '70s.*

Twyla kept waiting to categorize the woman as "hippie" and then to experience her in that classification. The judgment becomes a lens through which we see the person. A mother described the effects of being judged.

> *When I talk I can just see my son's eyes slightly close. Before he was a teenager he paid rapt attention to everything I said. Now, I think he hears about twenty percent of my words. The rest he dismisses because he figures whatever I am saying has a parental bias to it.*

If we have judged someone as selfish, we will tend to hear that person's offer to drive our child to school as having some self-serving purpose. We cannot hear any care for us in her offer. We have her "number" and generosity doesn't compute. When we have classified someone as incompetent, we don't have to listen to his plan for the project. We know already that it would be deficient. When we've labeled someone a "manipulator," we feel free to warn a friend, "Don't fall for what he says. He's just trying to get something out of you." A participant in a workshop we conducted commented about a member of the group, "I know I saw tears in his eyes and he said he was hurt, but he's such a tough guy I couldn't trust what he was saying."

As psychologists, we have heard frequent expressions of frustration and hurt from individuals who have been judged in their families in a way that makes it difficult or impossible to be heard. A young executive at a cosmetics company told us, "I dread going home. I am very respected at work. People, even my boss, are forever asking for my opinion. But at home I'm the dumb one. No one takes me seriously." A postal worker echoed her words: "I'm still seen as the troublemaker by my parents and sisters. I've had this job for fifteen years, but they still see me as a screw-up. I can't tell them anything—they wouldn't pay any attention." Most of us want to defend judgments as simply accurate depictions of others; yet, all of us have endured the hurt and exasperation of being judged in a way that denies us the chance to be heard and known.

Managers in business have the task of judging and evaluating their employees. Professionals, especially in the health care field, are trained to diagnose and to label their patients. They need to be particularly alert to the threat that such judging can be to understanding the individual. For example, a manager remarks impatiently to his administrative assistant, "I don't need all the details, just give me the gist of the problem." He cuts short anything else that she believes is necessary to be said. He has her slotted into the category of "excessive talking subordinate," and he doesn't have to listen to people in this category. To his boss, on the other hand, he listens for hours. Another manager judges one of her division heads to be "flat-footed and overly cautious—not one to make things happen." She might be quite perceptive in her observation, but she needs to be careful not to dismiss an expression of concern from the division head about a project as "just another case of being excessively prudent."

Professionals are often experienced as poor listeners, possibly because they evaluate, diagnose, and judge in a way that can devalue careful attention to the individual. For example, Clarissa is fearful that her physician won't listen with a fresh perspective.

Clarissa sat in her doctor's office for the fifth time this year. She felt a wave of despair as she began to describe her symptoms. She needed to convince her physician that this time the feelings of fatigue and pain were different. If he understood the new feelings, maybe he could figure out a diagnosis that would lead to treatment and relief. Having seen Clarissa four times previously and hearing the same complaints each time, the doctor was convinced that her symptoms were typical of lupus and saw nothing new. Each time she described her symptoms, he remarked, "You told me that last time." "Don't worry about that. The blood tests didn't indicate any problem there." "We're all getting older and feel those twinges."

Clarissa felt as if she were trying to communicate through an impenetrable fog. Indeed she was—the fog of judgment in the physician's mind. It could well be that his conviction was accurate. On the other hand, his diagnosis precluded any attention to the patient's distress, description of "new" symptoms, and desperation for relief. The judgment blocked out any data that did not fit the diagnosis.

An attorney described a phone call that he received from a new client.

I barely answered the phone before the woman on the other end started crying, pleading that I see her that day. I had this immediate impression of a way-too-needy person who would be calling me often and at any hour. I could picture someone who would be resisting my legal advice and questioning my bill. I told her I couldn't see her for a couple of weeks. I was actually booked, but I know that my instant impression of her didn't make me too open to shifting my schedule.

A teacher remarked, "I can tell in the first half hour of the first day of school which kids are going to be a joy to work with and which ones will give me trouble." How open to listening to these children will this teacher be once she has judged so quickly and unquestioningly? She will be looking for information to support her early judgments. The teacher is like a biased researcher who starts her exploration with a conclusion and looks through her research for data to confirm that conclusion rather than examining the data to decide what conclusion the data dictate. Effective teachers, like effective researchers, listen humbly and honestly, ready to learn, open to discover. Judgment can prevent such open-minded listening.

When we judge or diagnose, we not only affect our ability to hear the unique individual whom we are judging, we also fail to hear ourselves. We can think, particularly as professionals and managers, that we are objectively categorizing the person on the basis of observed facts. The patient is low in energy, has frequent thoughts of death, sleeps poorly, and occasionally thinks suicidal thoughts. Diagnosis: Depression. The worker is critical of his boss and refuses to perform assigned tasks. Judgment: Insubordinate. The student disturbs other students, fidgets, and is easily distracted. Judgment: Troublemaker or has Attention Deficit Disorder. We like to think that our judgments are objective and that they define accurately the reality of the individual involved. We don't realize that behind our judgments are

> When we judge or diagnose, we not only affect our ability to hear the unique individual whom we are judging, we also fail to hear ourselves.

feelings and needs that are often unattended. Clarissa's doctor is probably unaware that he might be feeling impatient and even irritated. These feelings can color his judgment and affect his ability to listen to her. The lawyer so quick to pronounce a potential client as "way too needy" might have feelings of annoyance and a memory of past resentments that are prompting his assessment. The teacher's judgment of "troublemaker" can hide her own feelings of anxiety about keeping classroom order. We judge someone as arrogant, not aware of our feelings of annoyance or hurt toward the individual. We call a colleague "brilliant" due to the feelings of respect and admiration that we have toward her. We say an acquaintance is selfish because we feel disappointed that they did not volunteer for a project that we are organizing. We might judge less if we first listened to and admitted our own feelings. Instead of burdening our child with a judgment of "bad boy" or "selfish" or "lazy" or even "brilliant" or "good girl," we could admit and express our feelings of frustration, disappointment, hurt, concern, or appreciation.

The next section of the book will discuss the importance of listening to ourselves as the prerequisite to understanding others. But at least for now we can realize that judging others can make it very difficult to hear them in their individual differences and specialness. We can also learn that when we look outward at another to judge, we frequently fail to listen inwardly to hear our feelings that are triggering the judgment.

Agreement or Disagreement: Another Form of Non-Listening

Listening is sometimes confused with agreeing or disagreeing with the speaker. At our communications workshops, some participants will resist listening with the objection, "If I listen, he'll think I am agreeing with him." Agreeing or disagreeing are not listening behaviors. They are a kind of judging or evaluating of the content of the speaker's words. In a counseling session this couple reacted to one another by disagreeing. Listening was employed only to hear perceptions of one another that could then be rebutted.

Kathleen: When I told him that the penalty for our taxes was due on the fifteenth, he exploded and blamed me for not having them ready on time.

Kevin: First of all, you didn't tell me we had to pay the penalty on the fifteenth. You said our taxes were due then. I don't agree that I exploded or blamed you. That's the way you see it.

Whatever Kathleen was feeling about Kevin's reaction about the penalty deadline, Kevin didn't hear. He heard information that he disputed. He disagreed with her statement that she had informed him of the deadline, and he disagreed with her description of his behavior. Kevin has judged Kathleen as wrong. It is easy to imagine that conversation deteriorating further into an argument of escalating disagreement.

In the following example, a young wife doesn't listen to her husband's frustration and need for sleep. She hears his plan regarding the children and objects.

Michael: We have to make sure that when we put the kids to bed they have to stay there for the night. No getting up for a glass of water. No coming into our room. Otherwise, they lose TV time. I have to get to sleep by ten if I'm going to function all day at work.

Martha: I don't think that's fair to the kids. I don't want them to be prisoners in their beds. You can't make rules for them like that.

Whatever Michael and Martha decide about the issue of their children's bedtime routines, they need to listen to one another's feelings and needs. Disagreement has to succumb to respectful attention to each other or no peaceful resolution will be attained, nor will they grow in closeness regarding issues involving the children. While they and the children are young, they need to learn to listen.

We can get so caught up in agreement or disagreement that we have trouble listening even to a compliment. Charlene says to her friend Ruth, "You always look so composed and organized. How can I compete with you when I live in utter chaos?" It is difficult for Ruth to listen to a friend who sounds as though she is giving her a compliment while at the same time being critical of herself. Ruth can fear that any listening would seem to give tacit agreement to both observations. Yet, if she would focus on and listen to Charlene's feelings of admiration, rather than trying to agree or disagree, she could gracefully acknowledge her friend's affirmation.

If listening is confused with agreement, then there is much that we will be unable to hear. If as we listen to the views and opinions of others we are prepared to respond only with agreement or disagreement, we will argue or we will fear that our silence is heard as tacit approval or sullen disagreement. Listening to another's feelings, perceptions, beliefs, and opinions goes beyond saying "yea or nay." It focuses instead on trying to understand the individual who is having these feelings and views. Listening offers to another what we wish for ourselves when we speak—respectful understanding.

R e f l e c t i o n Q u e s t i o n s

◉ Think of an occasion when you judged someone. What were you feeling toward this person? What did you need from this person?

◉ What is your immediate reaction when you sense that someone is judging you? Do you listen or respond by defending yourself?

◉ Under what circumstances do you need to be most vigilant to avoid judging others?

PART THREE

So How Do You *Listen?*

Getting to know you.
Getting to know all about you.

—*The King and I*
by Rogers and Hammerstein

CHAPTER TWELVE

Learning to
Listen
to
Ourselves

When we begin to identify our bad habits that prevent us from listening and start to resist these behaviors, then we are ready to change, ready to listen. We soon learn how difficult it is to break these habits and what enormous resolve is necessary to succeed. Despite our best intentions, the first time we hear criticism we jump to defend ourselves. The moment someone begins to narrate an incident, we are ready with our "me too" response. We still want to help with our advice and to get our response ready when the speaker is talking. It takes concentrated effort to break our old habits. Learning to listen takes full commitment.

The effort, however, is completely worthwhile. Listening is incredibly rewarding. We become more disciplined in our conversations. We avoid time-wasting, frustrating interchanges. We eliminate the futile arguments that exhaust us and that create distance and tension between us and those we love. We learn to understand more deeply our spouse, child, friend, relative, boss, and colleague. Trusting that they will be understood, these persons tell us more about themselves. They confide in us. They share their thoughts and hopes, dreams and problems. We learn to appreciate their particular reasons for acting the way that they do. We come to know how they feel about themselves, about us, about life. We learn that some of our judgments and perceptions of them need to be corrected. We grow closer to those we love and those with whom we work. Our effort to listen is greatly rewarded.

So how do you listen? We have stressed in the first two sections in this book that in order to listen you must focus on the speaker and on the *speaker's* feelings and needs, on what the *speaker* is trying to communicate. Ironically, in order to listen, to understand *the other*, you have to learn to listen first to *yourself. If you are not attentive to your own life experience, your own inner world of feelings, needs, and dreams, how can you possibly hear someone else's?* You might think that you would have no problem hearing a friend's excitement at getting a new job. But you are able to understand only if you have registered your own feelings in a similar situation. For example:

◆ the relief you felt at finding a job after weeks or months of unemployment

◆ the freedom you felt leaving a job that didn't challenge you or reward you as you moved on to a much more promising challenge

◆ the happiness you felt getting away from a boss or fellow workers that you didn't like or who didn't like you

♦   the pleasure of being in a new setting with new people,
    with new responsibilities

♦   the satisfaction of being chosen for a job over several
    others who were valued prospects

♦   the gratification of being able to earn more money to pay
    bills, buy a new car, renovate a house.

In order to empathize you do not need to have had the
identical experience of the speaker. All of us have not won
the lottery or lost a child. But you can listen to a friend's
excitement at unexpected happiness or unbearable grief if
you have celebrated your own delight in good news and
allowed yourself to feel profound sorrow at loss.

If you have not allowed yourself to feel the emotions of
starting something new or of ending an anxious period of
waiting, or of being selected for a position that you desire,
then when a friend shares his job news, you can
congratulate him but not really empathize. Listening to your
own experience and to your own feelings can prepare you
not to say "me too" but to listen attentively and
appreciatively to the experience of someone else.

When a sister talks of her fear of aging, you are prepared
to understand if you have registered your disappointment at
seeing wrinkles in your face and gray in your hair. If you
have been humbly aware of younger, attractive individuals
not noticing you as you have been admired in the past; if
you have been surprised to be called "sir" or "ma'am"; if
you have noticed a sagging where you want firmness,
bulging when you want thinness, and thinness where you
want a full muscular look, you can better hear her
trepidation about growing old.

Many of us deny our feelings because they are too threatening.
A man with a flushed face roars, "I'm not angry," and a
woman with a white-knuckled grip on the chair announces,
"I'm not afraid of going on interviews." We have heard

individuals deny most emotions: envy, fear, anger, hurt, confusion, or sadness. Unless you are free to admit your emotions, to know their power, and to recognize the behaviors that these feelings compel, then their depth, their subtlety, your discomfort with them, and your ignorance of them will make listening impossible. If you haven't acknowledged your disappointment at a lost opportunity; if you haven't admitted your envy of a colleague's success, your hurt at a friend's remark, your anger at a spouse's indifference, your sadness at a relative's death, then you are not equipped to empathize with another person's feelings. To begin effective listening, you not only need the patience, humility, and skill to listen to the speaker, you must first give attention to and be receptive to your own feelings. If you cannot admit your own feelings, you are incapable of understanding the feelings of others.

If you cannot admit your own feelings, you are incapable of understanding the feelings of others.

We are usually quite aware of what we are thinking. Psychologists who study such phenomena report that the average person has 50,000 thoughts per day. Some of us get stuck on one thought and obsess over it. Ask anyone what he or she is thinking and you will almost always get an answer. Feelings are in a different realm altogether. Ask most people what they are feeling and they will look at you as though you've accused them and answer, "Nothing, why?" Yet, you are feeling all the time, just as you are having 50,000 thoughts. The difference, however, is that while you are usually conscious of your thoughts, you might not be aware of your feelings.

Your education has trained you to think and taught you to value your opinions and thoughts. Too often your emotional world has been neglected. Until you learn to listen to your feelings, to put words on them, they exist outside of your awareness. But you do have these feelings and you have to learn to identify them.

Keeping a Notebook

There are myriad ways of raising awareness of your feelings, needs, motives, beliefs, and values. Meditation, for example, slows down the minds of its practitioners and allows time to become peacefully aware. Yoga, through tension-relaxing body positions, serves a similar goal. Praying, walking, resonating with nature, listening to music, and journaling are other ways of slowing down and tuning in to what you experience and what you value.

An exercise that you may find helpful in growing more aware of your feelings is to keep a feelings notebook. Take a few minutes each morning to write down the feelings that you have had to that point in the day. What did you feel getting up? Driving to work or walking the children to the bus stop? At a morning meeting? Doing the chores? Were you feeling tense or relaxed? Energetic or lethargic? Interested or bored? If you can't identify specific feelings, try general ones: were you feeling up or down? Close to the people you were with or distant? Feeling warmly toward these people or cold? Repeat this task at lunchtime and then again in the afternoon and evening. Or choose one particular time during the day to reflect on your feelings throughout the day. The purpose is to learn to focus attention on your inner world of emotions. In this way you become accustomed to bringing your feelings more clearly to mind and identifying them with words that are as accurate and descriptive as possible. Learning to label feelings can be like learning a new vocabulary. (A list of feelings can be found at the end of the book.)

A lawyer expressed his surprise at the effectiveness of the exercise.

I take pride in having a good vocabulary, but when I started keeping a notebook, I was able to identify very few feelings. Some days I would write nothing. I would think that possibly I had no feelings. Gradually, I started becoming aware of a whole gamut of emotions. It is amazing to me how out of touch with myself I actually was.

Even if you cannot get yourself to write down your feelings, taking a few minutes to ask yourself how you feel after a meeting, after a phone call, or after a conversation can help you to realize what emotions the particular event stirred in you. You might also become more aware of your feelings by trying to identify feelings that you have at particular times and toward specific people and events. How do you feel, for example,

+ on rainy days? (sad, cozy, content, melancholy)

+ when it snows? (excited, frustrated, eager, elated)

+ when your child goes to school? (lonely, delighted, anxious, proud)

+ toward snakes? (frightened, disgusted, fascinated)

+ toward kittens? (warm, amazed, protective, amused)

+ toward modern art? (suspicious, intrigued, wonder, distaste)

+ toward action movies? (inspired, revolted, aroused, bored)

+ when you pay bills? (scared, satisfied, proud, worried)

+ when your mother calls? (delighted, appreciative, irritated, surprised)

+ toward the president?
  (admiration, distrust, incredulous, respectful)

+ when you travel alone?
  (contented, stimulated, lonesome, wary)

+ when you travel by plane?
  (afraid, excited, alert, comfortable)

+ when you are in a large crowd?
  (panicky, disgruntled, excited)

+ when you have to speak publicly?
  (confident, terrified, reluctant)

Turn the radio off in the car and reflect on your feelings. Sit for a minute in silence to become more aware of your inner state. Close out the noise around you and even the noise of the thoughts within to become more conscious of what you feel.

Identifying the Feelings Behind Your Judgments

You can learn to know yourself by starting with what you know and then moving on to what is unknown. For example, you probably know your judgments but don't know what is happening within you that prompts the judgment. In this exercise, begin by judging someone, for instance, your best friend.

Judgment of Friend: Loyal or Generous

Now move into the less known. Behind every judgment there is a feeling. When you say "loyal," for instance, you are having an emotion that inclines you to make that judgment. You might feel trustful or safe or respected. When you call your friend "generous," the feeling you are having could be grateful or admiring. When you judge your friend as "talented," the emotion you are having might be respect or envy or awe. You can learn to identify your feelings toward the people in your life—boss, spouse, sibling, minister—by stating to yourself the judgment that you have made of them and then proceeding to your emotion.

You can then grow to know yourself further by identifying the need that you have of the person that you have judged. Feelings toward the person come from needs that he or she meets or does not meet. For example, suppose you have judged your friend loyal and have identified that you feel trust toward and safe with this friend. What need might you have that is being met to induce feelings of safety and trust? It might be that you have a need not to be hurt or betrayed, a need to be secure with a friend. The need is met so you feel trusting and safe.

Reflection on your feelings and needs can be heightened in the following exercise. List the significant people in your life, then indicate your judgment, the feelings that produce the judgment, and then your needs that in being satisfied or not provoke your feelings.

	Judgment	Feelings	Needs
Spouse			
Friend			
Boss			
Sibling			
Mother			
Father			

Noticing How Your Body and Actions Reveal Your Feelings

The judgments that you form can reveal you to yourself. You can hear through them to your feelings and needs. Your body and your behaviors are likewise sources of discovery of your emotional world. A headache can be a telltale sign that you are anxious and tense. For some a backache is a sure sign of repressed anger; for others it signifies nervousness or sadness. Some tremble when they are nervous or when they are angry; others stiffen their necks and shoulders. The stomach can point to emotions, as can dry mouth or perspiring hands. You have to listen to your body. It can communicate considerable data about your emotional state.

Your actions can also tell you what you are feeling. A vivacious young woman said, "I always know that I'm feeling nervous or insecure when I start talking too much." Another person said, "My voice gets louder when I feel unsure of myself." Others become very quiet when they feel uncomfortable. A slightly overweight woman told us, "If I find myself going for a cookie, I realize that I'm feeling either hurt or lonely." Reaching for a cigarette can telegraph certain emotions as can eating very quickly, driving fast, or extra slowly, needing a drink, or needing to clean the kitchen. Delaying your taxes, not returning a phone call, putting off a project, losing your keys—all these behaviors are trying to tell you to become aware of what you are feeling.

Sharing Your Feelings
Clarifies Your Feelings

You can also become aware of your feelings by trying to express them to someone who will listen. The more that you speak in the language of feelings the more skilled you will become at identifying them. When you speak a foreign language frequently, the vocabulary of that language becomes readily available to you. Similarly, when you regularly express your feelings, words that describe these feelings are at your command. One couple adopted the practice of sitting down each evening with one another for half an hour to share the feelings they had expressed during the day. They described their experience.

At first, we would feel as if we had nothing to say after about five minutes. It was pretty awkward. We'd end up talking about the kids, but after awhile we had lots of feelings to share. We even looked forward to getting together to tell them to each other. Writing them down during the day helped but mainly just making ourselves talk this way every night has made it natural.

When we consult with organizations we encourage each member of the group, whether the organization is a business or a civic or academic society, to choose a "buddy" to whom he or she can vent or express whatever emotions are being felt. The point of the exercise is not to gossip but to release and to clarify emotions. The practice also teaches the participants to come to know themselves and to know one another. The psychologist Sidney Jourard emphasized in his book, *The Transparent Self*, that when we identify the feelings that are often hidden within us and then put these feelings out to another person, we come to realize who we are. Self-revelation becomes self-understanding. *Unless we understand ourselves, we are not able to understand anyone else.*

Knowing Your Feelings When You Are Trying to Listen

Unless you know your feelings, you cannot know someone else's. Unless you know what you are feeling at the moment when you attempt to listen, that feeling will scuttle your effort. For example, a mother is committed to hear her teenager.

Teenager Says: I want to drop algebra. I'm not getting it, and anyway, I'm too far behind.

Mother Feels:

Concern—that her child is running away from a challenge.

Anxious—that the decision will hurt her chances of getting into college.

Irritated—that her daughter has gotten behind in her class work.

Mother Reacts: You can't always take the easy way in life. You talk to the teacher and find a way to catch up. Maybe you need special help.

If the mother is going to listen to her daughter before responding, she will need to realize quickly that she is feeling concern, anxiety, and irritation. Then she will have to resist reacting, "hold" her feelings for the moment, and attempt to understand her daughter's feelings. Later, she can share her own feelings with her daughter. Of course, she can only share her feelings if she knows them. The mother can only resist reacting if she can first register her feelings so that they do not propel her annoyed reaction.

The husband in the following example needs to be conscious of what he is feeling himself, if he is going to hear his wife.

Wife Says: We need to get away this summer with the kids. We haven't been away as a family for ages.

Husband Feels:

Annoyed—at his wife's accusatory tone.

Anxious—at what kind of trip she is contemplating.

Worried—at the potential cost of the trip.

Husband Reacts: It wasn't ages ago. We went to the Cape to visit your father last fall. I think the kids want to stay home with their friends this summer.

The husband's feelings rule the day, keep him from listening to his wife, and probably provoke an argument. Like the mother of the teenager wanting to drop a course and the husband reacting to his wife about a family vacation, you will fail to listen if you don't become more alert to your feelings.

Knowing the Feelings That You Have Difficulty Hearing

The president of a large paper company told his top aides, "Don't bring me bad news! I don't want to hear it." His directive may or may not have demonstrated creative management, but at least it expressed awareness of what he couldn't hear. We all have limits as to what we can hear or at least to what we can hear without real difficulty. A woman who has been hospitalized with major depression was asked months later if she would be willing to talk to a young man who was feeling very low. She declined, saying, "I'm sorry, but I can't hear anyone who is depressed. It's too close to what I've been through." The paper company executive was seemingly feeling too discouraged or too anxious about the company to listen to any negative news. The woman recovering from a depressive episode knew that listening to the young man 's feelings could plunge her back into depression. There are probably feelings that you have trouble hearing. Knowing yourself allows you to acknowledge your limits. Sometimes this admission can free you to explore these limits and get beyond them. A counselor whom we were supervising told us, "Until you pointed it out, I wasn't aware that I steered the client away from talking about his sister's death. I think that whole issue is tough for me. My little brother died when I was twelve and my mother was never the same." To be effective in his career, the counselor needed to explore at length the feelings that he harbored about his brother's death and his mother's reaction. It might not be easy for you to hear someone's feelings of joy if you are feeling sad; to hear feelings of physical accomplishment if you are sick; feelings of anger if your parents were violent; feelings regarding success if you feel like a failure. Awareness of the difficulty you have in listening to specific feelings can point to parts of your lives that you need to examine. At least, the awareness can enable you to be more self-accepting of your limitations as a listener.

Listening is so challenging that it demands all of your attention.

Listening is so challenging that it demands all of your attention. You have to know yourself even to be aware at any moment whether or not you are listening. Your child can be talking to you, and you can seem to be listening saying, "That's nice," or, "Yes, that must have been exciting." But unless you are tuned into yourself, you can be on "automatic pilot." You can be saying all the right things but be miles away, not present at all. The way that you are feeling, the mood that you happen to be in, can make you more defensive than open to listening, and more preoccupied than attentive. *Self-awareness is a prerequisite for being able to listen.*

R e f l e c t i o n   Q u e s t i o n s

@ Do you have a plan for heightening your awareness to your own feelings, needs, motives, beliefs and values?

@ Which of your own behaviors or physical reactions alert you to feelings you are having?

@ What feelings directed at you by others are the hardest for you to "hear"?

CHAPTER THIRTEEN

Learning to *Listen* to Others

First and foremost, when listening to another person your focus needs to be on that person. You are not planning your reaction to what the person is saying; you are not preparing your advice or your defense or your opinion. If you picture a spotlight hanging above you and the speaker, its light would be shining on him or her, not on you. You are looking at the other, alert to the other's words, the other's feelings, the other's message. You are alert to tone of voice, emphasis, choice of words, and facial expression. You are attempting to hear what he or she is trying to communicate. You are attentive to the other's body language—slumped shoulders, tapping fingers, tight mouth, relaxed shoulders—realizing that the speaker is communicating through his body language as well as by words. Sometimes you will hear feelings expressed through tone of voice more than through words. Sometimes the speaker's flushed face or trembling hands will convey emotions veiled by words. When you listen, you focus on the whole person. You are alert, aware, and receptive to the speaker.

Such focused attention is difficult to maintain; such receptivity is not easy. Even when we attempt to listen to music, for instance, to savor the emergence of a symphony's themes, to register the interaction between instruments, to hear the songwriter's meaning in the lyrics, our minds can drift. We get distracted. We stop listening. But when we do stay focused on the music, we connect with it in a way that nourishes and delights. Your attitude in listening to a person needs to have that quality of attentive receptivity. At the moment of listening, you have eyes and ears only for the speaker. If the central message of the speaker is an expression of emotion, you listen for the feelings: excitement, hurt, fear, anger. If the speaker is primarily attempting to impart information, you try to grasp clearly the data expressed. You are not at the moment of listening attempting to evaluate the information or to control the speaker's feelings. You are open to receive feelings, message, or information. Your goal is to listen and to understand.

> At the moment of listening, you have eyes and ears only for the speaker.

Paraphrase What You Have Heard

The questions to ask yourself as you listen are:

+ What am I hearing?

+ What feelings am I hearing?

+ What is the message?

+ What is the information that I am hearing?

The next step is to offer back to the speaker in your own words what you have heard. This offering back should have a questioning tone suggesting that you are checking to see if what you are hearing is what the speaker is trying to say. You don't presume that what you have heard is necessarily what the speaker intends to communicate. When you offer back what you have heard, the speaker has the opportunity to clarify or to expand on what he or she is saying. For example,

> **Child**: Camp stinks this year. It's not like last year. The counselors don't care. Some of the kids are really mean.

> **Father**: You sound disappointed that camp is different this year and not as nice as it was last year, as if you were hoping that you would be as close to the counselors as you were to Brianna last summer? And it sounds as if you felt hurt by some of the kids?

> **Note**: The father refrains from expressing feelings of fear that he will have to find another camp or child-care situation, impatience with the child's complaints, fears about the child's social skills. He is not trying to convince the child that things will get better. The father is not giving the child advice or giving a lesson on perseverance. Instead, he listens.

He tells the child, in his own words, what he believes the child is telling him.

Child: Yeah, I thought Brianna was going to be there, and she always made Tommy stop playing dodge ball if he hit too hard.

Father: Are you afraid you won't be able to stop Tommy yourself?

Child: Tommy's mean. He doesn't care if he hurts people, and he doesn't play the game right.

Father: Sounds like you're scared Tommy won't play by the rules and you'll get hurt.

Child: Yeah, I'm going to tell the counselor she should tell us all the rules again before we play.

Note: Parents, in particular, need to listen, especially when they hear a child in need. By listening they provide space for the child to figure out how to solve his or her own problems. The father learns that by listening first, his concerns—new camp, different child care situation, social skills lesson—are put to rest.

In order to listen to the child, the father quickly had to be aware of his own feelings of concern that his child sounded sad or his fear that the child would want to drop out of camp. He had to discipline himself to "hold" his feelings and the reactions that these feelings might prompt. *Listening calls for self-control.* When everything in the caring or frightened parent wants to solve the problem with advice, checking this impulse and continuing "simply" to listen takes great effort.

Hold It! Don't React

....

Listening, then, demands that you be alert to your own feelings and then that you say to yourself, "Hold it!" *Refrain from sharing your own feelings for the moment.* This is not to say that you deny your feelings or suppress them. For the moment, though, "tuck them under your arm" and first confirm that you have really heard the speaker. Your feelings have been stirred by what you *think* you have heard from the speaker. By exercising the "hold it" you have time to play back your understanding of the speaker's thoughts, feelings, and needs. You might have heard correctly or you might be way off the mark. The speaker now has the opportunity to confirm or clarify his words. After listening, the feelings that you "held" might have changed. If the father in the example had not "held" his feelings of fear that his daughter wanted to leave camp, he would have spent his time trying to convince her to stay at camp when she had no intention of leaving.

Countless interactions result in wasted words, wasted time, and needless frustration because the "listener" presumed that he or she understood what was being said, and then reacted. A conscious "hold it" response saves time and energy and results in more satisfying meeting for both sides. The following examples portray individuals practicing the skill of "holding" feelings and reactions until they have listened.

Example #1

> **Husband**: Have you any idea what it is like to get up at 5:00 a.m. every morning to get the train for the city? I can't keep this up.

> **Note**: If the wife hears a judgment of her that she is oblivious to or unappreciative of the burden that

daily commuting is for him, then she might feel impatience, anger, or resentment. If she hears that he might quit his job then she might feel very anxious. Any and all of these feelings she will have to "hold" if she is going to listen in a way that communicates understanding and in a manner that clarifies for her what he is feeling.

Wife: I know that you are worried that you're feeling more tired these days and the commute is getting to you. You never planned on being a commuter and it sounds like you're frustrated that you have been doing it so long and don't see an end to it.

Note: In listening the wife is trying to empathize with her husband's feelings. She is not focused on what he might be saying about her. If he is angry with her then she will try to understand. But if she doesn't stop to listen, she will hear only judgments of her and will react. Later she may need to share her own feelings, but first she has to listen to his.

Example #2

Veronica: I'm not going to talk to Candice anymore. She makes me so mad when she brags about her business trips to France.

Note: If Sheri, the listener, hears only blame of Candice, she will have to "hold" her feelings of protectiveness for her friend Candice. If she hears that Veronica abandons friends too easily, she will have to "hold" feelings of impatience.

Sheri: It sounds like it gets you down when Candice describes her latest trip, and you wish you could be going on a business trip to France yourself.

Note: Sheri has not admonished Veronica about blaming a friend or scolded her about dumping friends. In focusing on Veronica's feelings rather than on her own impatience or protectiveness, Sheri can hear Veronica's sadness about not being able to travel and maybe her jealousy of Candice. Whether she heard correctly or not, she is more likely to connect with Veronica than if she had scolded. Once she has heard her friend, she might want to share her feelings of protectiveness of Candice.

Example #3

Sister: I'm afraid that if we go on vacation with your wife and kids, we won't be able to just lie on the beach. You always like to be going and doing.

Note: If the brother in this example hears blame of his family for spoiling his sister's vacation or a judgment of himself as "hyperactive," then he will need to "hold" feelings of resentment and irritation.

Brother: It sounds like you want to be sure that we spend a number of days of the vacation just relaxing and not have to worry about getting all involved in making plans.

Note: By not defending or allowing his vulnerability to govern his words, the brother listened to his sister in a way that validated her vacation needs. When the conversation continues he might need to share feelings of irritation at what he has heard as to her judgment of him and of his family.

Example #4

> **Boss**: I need this report by Friday, but I would like to see a rough draft of it by Tuesday so I can see if we have all the data in it that we need for the meeting on Monday.

> **Note**: If the employee hears that his boss lacks confidence in her, she might feel fear for her job. She will have to "hold" her feelings of fear and the defense that she might be tempted to give.

> **Employee**: Let me make sure I have these dates in my calendar correctly. I'll give you the rough copy on Tuesday so we can make sure we have all the figures right, and then I'll give you the final copy on Friday so we can do one more check before you go to the meeting on Monday.

> **Note**: In this instance, the employee is recognizing the boss's concern for accuracy and then clarifying his instructions. The focus is on the boss, not on what she fears might be his perceptions of her.

Example #5

> **Mother-in-law**: I think the dinner arrangements would work much better if the children had their own separate table.

> **Note**: The daughter-in-law has to "tuck under her arm" her feelings of defensiveness and impatience if she hears criticism either of her ability to plan a dinner party or of her children's manners.

> **Daughter-in-law**: You sound like you are concerned that the children would disrupt the adults and that

the children would be happier anyway if they ate by themselves.

Note: It might be that by clarifying her mother-in-law's needs the daughter-in-law's feelings of defensiveness and impatience fade away. If she has heard her mother-in-law clearly and yet she still wants to arrange the seating differently, it is now her turn to speak and hope her mother-in-law can listen.

There are two times in particular when you are challenged to "hold" your reaction and to listen: when you are given a compliment and when you are criticized. For some people, a compliment can cause such embarrassment or awkwardness as to make listening nearly impossible. For others, feelings of hurt or defensiveness can impede any effort to hear criticism.

Example #1

Brian: Congratulations! Your presentation was excellent!

Note: Luis, Brian's colleague, has to check his tendency to cover his embarrassment by reacting, "I don't know. I didn't think I was very clear."

Luis: I appreciate your telling me. Thank you.

Luis might be far too flustered to try to paraphrase feelings of respect that he hears from Brian, but at least he can refrain from rejecting the words of praise and try to accept graciously Brian's compliment.

Example #2

Luther to his date: Hey, you look beautiful tonight.

Note: Demi had to "hold" her feelings of awkwardness and fear that Luther might think that she is conceited if she pays too much attention to his compliment.

Demi: What a nice thing to say. Thank you.

Demi lets Luther know that she is hearing and accepting his affirmation. His gift is acknowledged and received. She even affirms him for giving the compliment.

Sometimes connection can be made between listener and speaker by hearing the feelings that are behind the compliment.

Example #3

Delia: Jerry, I haven't told you how grateful I am for the way you've been taking care of Mom and Dad. You've been a godsend to them.

Note: Jerry has to "hold" his self-consciousness. He has to restrain himself from making any remarks that would deflect the compliment; such as, "No problem. I've got the time." or "I probably should spend more time with them."

Jerry: I hear how much it means to you what I've been doing with Mom and Dad. It seems like it is a big relief to you that I can be here for them.

In hearing the feelings behind the compliment, Jerry can focus on his sister's feelings and hear what it is like for her that he has been caring for their parents. He hears her gratitude and her relief. He hears her feelings, not just a compliment about him.

We need to be noticed, complimented, and acknowledged with praise. Yet, it can be very difficult to drink in the very affirmation that we so need. We fear being viewed as vain. We feel awkward or embarrassed. Learning to receive the offering of complimentary words allows us to accept the nourishment that affirmation provides. Such reception also graciously acknowledges the gift and the giver. It is satisfying for the person offering the compliment to have it received. Hearing a compliment rejected or deflected, on the other hand, can make the giver feel foolish. The rejection can convey a message that the compliment (and the one offering it) is not regarded as sincere.

Personal development requires constructive criticism. You won't grow while stuck in non-productive or hurtful behaviors you don't see. But being open to such criticism demands that you "hold" defensive reactions.

Example #1

Mel (manager): Patrick, your production has been outstanding, but you are hurting and angering people that you work with. You have got to be more sensitive.

Note: Patrick is hurt. He feels that he has performed at peak levels while those around him have done very little. He has to "hold" his retort, "It would be easy to be sensitive if I didn't have to ride herd on these guys to get anything done."

Patrick: I appreciate your comments. I'm glad that you can see I'm getting results. I want to really produce. I need to hear more from you about how you are seeing me as insensitive. I'm sure that I can improve the way I talk to the guys.

Example #2

> **Toby (son):** Mom, you are forever on my case. You're too critical. I never know what mood you'll be in, and you take it out on me. It's not fair.
>
> **Note:** Toby's mother has to "hold" her impatience and possibly her guilt in order for her to listen to Toby.
>
> **Mother:** I'm sorry that you are feeling as though I'm being critical. You must be hurt if you think that I've been taking my moods out on you and getting on your case.

By not countering with a list of Toby's behaviors that have warranted her criticism, his mom allows him to express his feelings. He might be hurt, angry, resentful. He might even be concerned about her moodiness. Only by "holding" her reaction will she give Toby the room to tell her all that he is feeling. Possibly, she will learn about herself. How her son is experiencing her can be a revelation that can urge her to look at her moods and at the way she handles them. She can also consider the manner in which she has been relating with Toby.

Example #3

> **Eva (girlfriend):** You never want to do anything with my friends. It always has to be with your friends. I like your friends, but just once I'd like to do something with mine.
>
> **Note:** Jamal has to "hold" his defense, "Never? Are you kidding me? Where were we last Friday night?" His reaction would precipitate an argument about who is right and who is wrong. Jamal would allow himself no time to reflect on his level of comfort or

discomfort at being with her friends. A quick reaction would not allow him to consider her view of him, her sense that the relationship is unbalanced, and that he is unappreciative of her sense of being at a disadvantage with his friends. Quick, defensive retorts permit little opportunity for self-reflection.

Jamal: You sound resentful. You seem to think that it always has to be my way, with my friends. You also sound hurt that I don't seem to be aware of what it's like for you. You feel like you're on the outside with my friends. You've known them only a short time while I've known them forever.

Jamal's remarks allow Eva to express her feelings and allow him to reflect on the way that he has been acting.

Criticism can help you to know yourself and to see yourself through the eyes of others. You won't necessarily agree with all of the observations that you hear, but by resisting the tendency to defend by explanation or by counterattack, you give yourself the opportunity for self-reflection and subsequent growth.

Be Patient! Learning to Listen Skillfully Takes Time

Paraphrasing requires skill as well as discipline. Paraphrasing requires skill as well as discipline. Some people object to offering back what they have heard the other say as sounding "artificial" or "awkward." Acquiring any skill subjects the learner to a period of clumsiness. The pianist doesn't start by playing brilliantly and subtly. To ski, play tennis, or speak a foreign language requires patience. To listen well, to communicate understanding, means that you have to endure feeling awkward or even being accused by others of sounding stilted or unreal. An agent at an insurance company told us:

> *When I started really listening to what people were saying and letting them know what I was hearing, some of the agents were critical or sarcastic. Now these same guys come into my office to talk about stuff that's bothering them. Listening in this way to my clients also has changed my business entirely.*

A single mother of teenage girls said,

> *My girls used to get on me about paraphrasing. Now if I don't let them know I'm hearing them, they'll say, "Mom, you're not listening!"*

The more skillful you become in letting those you relate with know what you are hearing, the less they notice your listening behavior. They know only the satisfaction of being heard.

Listen From Your Experience

When you listen, you can only truly understand the other person if you have had an experience that has some of the sense or feeling of the speaker's. For example, suppose you are trying to understand a friend's helplessness at being unable to convince her daughter that she is attractive and worthwhile. You need to tap into feelings you have had in seeing someone you love plagued by self-doubt or feelings of inferiority. It is important not to presume that your feelings of care, concern, or helplessness are identical to those of your friend. It is also important that you not fall into a "me too" non-listening trap. You do not shift the focus onto yourself. You do not refer to your similar experience. You simply reflect on the feelings you had in a potentially like circumstance as you listen. In so doing when you offer back to your friend what you are hearing, your listening will convey a depth of understanding as it is imbued with a genuine sense of empathy. As we said in the previous chapter, you cannot listen to another if you are not listening to yourself. As Alexander Solzhenitsyn wrote, "When you're cold don't expect sympathy from someone who's warm" (Epigraph, *One Day in the Life of Ivan Denisovich*).

Realistically, you cannot have had all of life's experiences. If you are male, for example, you have not carried a child within you or have given birth. But the more that you open yourself to life's wonders and terrors the more that you can understand someone else's joy and awe, fear and sadness. Consider the person to whom you would want to share your most profound thoughts, feelings, and experiences. The individual that you would choose will probably be the person that you perceive to have the wisdom, compassion, and tolerance that comes from living life fully.

Know Your Intention

Your intention in listening, in paraphrasing what you have heard is not to show others that you are skilled at a technique. Your aim is to fully understand the one speaking, to get into his shoes, to see things from her point of view. Letting the other know what you are hearing is a means, a very effective means, to that end. Without the goal of really understanding the other, paraphrasing would be a mechanical, even manipulative technique, provoking annoyance or distrust. Repeating back the words that you have heard in parrot-like fashion is meaningless—cute from Polly but annoying from anyone else. If you do not truly want to understand your child, spouse, friend, or employee at a given moment, don't repeat their words. But when you do want to understand, offering back what you have heard in your own words can help you to realize what you are hearing; at the same time you will be communicating to the speaker that you are trying to understand. By using your own words you avoid parrot-like repetition, while trying to get a real sense of what you are hearing from the speaker. No speaker wants to be the object of an empty technique, but if he or she trusts that you have a genuine intention to understand, even if your effort to listen is clumsy, it will be accepted and appreciated.

How Do You Know That You Have Understood?

Motivated by the intention to understand, to get into the shoes of the other, you offer back what you have heard. You can introduce your effort to listen with words such as,

♦ "What I hear you saying is . . ."

♦ "It sounds like you feel . . ."

♦ "Let me see if I have it clear . . ."

The words direct your focus as well as announce your intention to listen. Then you repeat back in your own words what you have heard. Your voice rises at the end of your offering indicating that you are checking with the speaker to confirm that what you are hearing is what he or she is intending to express. For example, "You sound irritated by what your boss said?" The voice rising communicates a checking to confirm, "Is that it?" rather than a declarative statement, "You are irritated by what your boss said." The voice dropping sounds more like a comment from the listener than a questioning, confirming response.

Your raised voice invites the speaker to confirm that you have heard correctly or to clarify or to expand on what he or she has said. As the speaker experiences understanding, hears herself echoed in your listening words, she will automatically nod her head in agreement or utter words like "exactly." If the speaker isn't nodding to your paraphrasing or saying "exactly," she is probably indicating not having been heard. Before you stop listening and begin to respond, it might be prudent to ask, "Do you feel that I have heard you?" Such a question would be particularly apt if you are not sure that you have understood or that the speaker has finished for the moment.

Understanding can be communicated by a wink, a smile, and a squeeze of the hand. Sometimes the most profound understanding can be expressed with no words at all. But that is a result of deep connection, a connection usually achieved by clear, attentive, dedicated verbal expression of understanding.

> Sometimes the most profound understanding can be expressed with no words at all.

Effects of Listening

Effect #1: Clarification

Few people say clearly and thoroughly what they intend to communicate in their first utterance. Studies, as we have noted, reveal that patients often don't express their major concerns initially in speaking to their doctor. All of us need time to express ourselves clearly. So, quick responses, reactions, or interruptions by the listener stifle further expression by the speaker. In the face of such reactions, the speaker has no opportunity to develop his thoughts or feelings for himself, let alone for the listener. When you offer back what you have heard, the speaker is given space to hear herself, to clarify her thoughts, to expand on her meaning. Listening then is a gift to the speaker, a gift that allows self-expression, self-clarification, and self-understanding. An executive told us,

So often at the start of a session I will have only a vague idea of what is bothering me, but as you listen I get clear on what it's about. I wish I could figure things out more by myself. I seem to need to talk things out before I realize all that I'm feeling. It makes me want to listen more to my direct reports — I guess my wife and kids, too.

We want to know ourselves, to understand our feelings, our needs, and our drives. Having a spouse, a friend, or a colleague who will listen provides us with the attention we need to come to know ourselves.

Effect #2: Connection

Maybe no man is an island, but you can often feel isolated, alone in your own sense of yourself. It is easy to feel cut off from others, lost in your doubts, or your fears. It is easy to feel different, inferior, afraid to be found out as inadequate. At work you can feel that you are in a silo removed from others; at home you can feel distant from those you need most. Being understood, really heard, can dispel the alienation. A recovering alcoholic, after being listened to at a meeting of Alcoholics Anonymous said, "I felt like I took a spaceship and landed in a place where I felt at home." Support groups like AA provide for many the understanding that they lack sometimes in their own families. These groups at their best do not judge or blame. They listen. You need to be heard and understood. You need to listen and to understand. Listening can be the bridge between you and your children, your spouse, family members, colleagues, and friends. A forty-eight-year-old nurse told us,

I can't tell you what it is like to be finally close to my sister. I had always judged her as selfish and not caring about the family. She'd always seen me as playing the "good girl" to our folks. When she got sick we started talking—no, started

*listening. I know her now like I never did. I understand why
she has kept to herself. And she has really heard me. What a
waste of time that we've been like strangers for years. But,
thank God, we are finally close.*

It is greatly satisfying for us, the authors, in doing
marriage counseling and family counseling, to see spouses
and family members come from behind defenses to stop
attacking and defending and to begin sharing openly and
listening effectively. It is rewarding when we consult with
organizations to watch workers leave their "silos" and begin
to understand, to appreciate, and to feel connected to one
another.

Effect #3: Trust

Trust is necessary in breaking down barriers between
individuals and groups. When you trust someone, your
defenses fall away and you open yourself and gravitate
toward that person. An essential characteristic of trust in someone is confidence that the person understands you. When he or she listens to you, understands you, appreciates you, we feel safe with that person. We trust. Much energy is expended protecting ourselves; playing roles that we hope will keep us safe. Playing the role of good daughter or competent homemaker takes effort, but, in the name of emotional safety, it can seem necessary to avoid criticism or to earn praise. Being an all-knowing dad or take-charge husband can be exhausting but can keep the vulnerable man armed against feelings of inadequacy or guilt. It is freeing

when you can let down your guard and be yourself. To do so you need to trust that you will not be judged and found wanting, but rather known, appreciated, and understood. The character Evelina in the play *Bloomer Girl* speaks of the joy experienced in such understanding:

> *He smiled understandingly . . . much more than understandingly. It was one of those rare smiles with a quality of external reassurance in it, that you may come across only once or twice in your lifetime. It faced—or seemed to face— the whole external world for an instant, and then concentrated on you with an irresistible prejudice in your favor. It understood you as you would like to believe in yourself, and assured you that it had precisely the impression of you that, at your best, you hoped to convey.*

You are fortunate if you have had or have a person so understanding of you. You are likewise blessed when you are able to listen with such wise understanding.

Effect #4: Intimacy

Listening has its most rewarding effect when it unites us deeply with the individuals in our lives whom we love most. It is so painful yet so common to be separated emotionally from those who mean the most to us. In the separation we refuse to listen and we are not heard. An argument with our spouse, partner, or child can drain us of energy. Not understanding our son, not being understood by our spouse can eclipse all else that is good in our life. But as much as lack of careful listening can cause agonizing distance, genuine, attentive understanding towards one or from one we love deeply can provide an intense sense of oneness.

The husband of a couple who have worked hard to identify areas of misunderstanding between them and who have learned to listen said,

We've never doubted that we love each other. But we see now just how far apart we were on a whole bunch of important issues. I had no idea what she felt about me as a dad, as a lover, or what she experienced when I got together with my brothers. I thought I understood how she felt about religion, even about how much I work. I was way off. We have talked through so many issues now. It's unbelievable how close we feel now—closer than we have ever been.

It is easy for distance to creep gradually between individuals: spouse, family members, friends who mean the world to each other. *Listening allows you to discover again the profound joy of intimate connection.* It makes physical contact a natural expression of closeness. It is not a one-time effort to listen closely. Development of intimacy requires that you commit yourself every day, around countless issues and circumstances, to stop, to focus, and to listen.

Effect #5: Self-Acceptance

Being listened to gives us space to hear ourselves, to clarify what we are trying to say, to sort ourselves out. It connects us with the person who understands us. Being understood fosters trust in us toward the one listening. It also frees us from feelings of alienation and aloneness. Mysteriously, being heard and understood also allows us to accept our feelings and ourselves. Feeling jealous of a friend's success causes us to feel guilt and self-dislike. Admitting these jealous feelings to someone who listens, who doesn't judge but who understands, can free us of the original jealousy as well as of the consequent self-dislike. When we can acknowledge out loud feelings that are difficult for us to admit such as anger, sexual attraction, a sense of inferiority, and be heard deeply and caringly, we find that we can accept the feelings and accept ourselves. The open admission of our feelings followed by non-judgmental empathy is a type of confessional experience that promotes healing and leads to peaceful self-acceptance.

We all have feelings that we would prefer not to experience. As someone wrote, "Who must not admit shamefacedly secret delight at the worst misfortune of the closest friend?" The Germans even have a word for such feelings, *schadenfreude*. (harming joy). These feelings harbored in secret can make us doubt our goodness and our ability to love. When a sympathetic listener can understand our feelings, we can begin to accept them ourselves and learn to resist condemning ourselves.

We not only have feelings that we find difficult to accept, we all regret actions that we have committed. We rue the moment that we lost our temper with our child, the time that we avoided people who deserved our attention, the occasions where we spoke hurtful words, drank too much, ate too much and loved too little. When we are able to admit our feelings of remorse to someone who listens, who understands, who accepts us, we become able to forgive ourselves and to accept that we are not perfect, but that we are also not evil.

We need the support of one another to believe that we are worthwhile. We need a friend, a spouse, and a relative to listen to us and to understand. Then we can pick ourselves up and continue to try to be our best selves. A wise person commented that the only difference between a saint and a sinner is that the saint doesn't give up. Maybe the saint experiences compassionate understanding and is able to accept it.

Each day that you listen to your child, your spouse, a family member with love, you help that person to accept himself or herself to be a bit more peaceful, a bit more hopeful. Such is the effect of an understanding word or smile. When someone really hears you just as you are, you are more able to know yourself and to appreciate yourself.

Listening, then, is possibly the ultimate gift. It says to the other that you are worth my full attention, that what you have to say is important to me, that what you experience matters to me. It is relatively easy to give many gifts, especially material ones. But to give your full attention, to enter into the world of your child, spouse, sibling, or friend, to understand, that gift demands that you take the focus off your own opinions and need, and concentrate solely on him or her. This gift is as special as it is rare. The most frequent and most painful complaint of spouses, of children, of parents is "You don't listen." "You don't understand." That which you need most from the key people in your life, you might not receive. Just as sadly, you frequently fail to give. But you can learn to listen. You can make listening to those key people a central value and commitment.

Reflection Questions

◉ Whom do you most want to listen to?

◉ When and how will you listen to this person or these persons?

◉ How can you practice this vital skill of listening?

CHAPTER FOURTEEN

Learning
to
Be Heard

It is in your power to listen. You can learn to control your old, non-listening habits and you can grow skillful in the art of listening. But you can feel utterly helpless in being heard yourself. You know how much you yearn to be heard by your boss, your doctor, your spouse, your parents, or your child. But if they are not listening to you, what can you do? *Telling others that they are not listening is usually unproductive.* Your accusation prompts them to defend themselves, to get angry, or to blame you for being too needy or too critical. You are no more heard in your complaint than you are in other interactions. Yet giving up the effort to be heard results in a dissatisfying, distant relationship. So what can you do to be heard?

There is no sure-fire answer. There is no magic wand that you can wave over other people that turns them into marvelous listeners. Instead of looking to the other people in your life to change, you can look to yourself. If you want to be listened to, you have a far better chance of that need being met if you change your own way of talking, if you stop expressing yourself in ways that tend to guarantee that you will not be heard. When you want a significant person in your life to get into your shoes, to hear your feelings, and to appreciate your experience, you will have scant hope of that empathy occurring if you are criticizing him or telling her what she should be doing. If you are focusing on the other in criticism or blame, you will probably trigger defensiveness, not understanding. You shouldn't be surprised that people do not understand your feelings if you avoid sharing them out of fear of being vulnerable. Just as you learned to identify your non-listening behaviors in Part Two, such as interrupting, advice giving, or judging, so, too, you need to become aware of your non-sharing ways of talking. Speaking personally, openly, honestly does not guarantee being heard. But speaking impersonally, critically, judgmentally makes being understood a very remote prospect.

Indirect Ways of Sharing: Judgments

In Chapter Twelve we stated that when you make a judgment, your feelings, needs, and perceptions are prompting the label that you fix on another. If you call your friend selfish, you might be feeling hurt or disappointed or envious depending on your need and your perception. If your need is for your friend to think of you when you are sick, you might feel hurt when she fails to call. You perceive her behavior as a failure to think of you while she meets her own needs. If you need her to help you with a project, you might feel disappointed at her refusal and again see her behavior as self-serving. If your need is to be more self-respecting and to learn to say "no" more confidently, you might envy your friend's freedom to say "no" so assertively.

Now suppose you want your friend to hear you in your feelings, your needs, and your perceptions. Telling her, "You know, Marie, you are really selfish," will provide little chance that you will be heard. You have focused on her and judged her. You have not directly shared with her the feelings you have toward her, the needs you have, the perceptions you have of her behavior. In a sense you have stayed hidden. You might think you were "just being honest," but in reality you have just been judgmental. Being honest would mean you have shared *your feelings* toward her. It would mean you have made *yourself* visible to her, brought your *feelings, needs, and perceptions* into the open. For example, "I felt hurt when you didn't call to see if I needed anything while I was sick." She might still not hear you. She might even hear your feelings as judgment of her. But at least you have admitted the feelings and needs and perceptions that you want her to hear. To hide them behind a judgment while hoping that she hears them would seem folly, particularly when you know how difficult it is to listen. Note the difference between judgments and personal sharing of self in the following:

Judgments *Speaker is invisible*	*Direct Sharing* *Speaker is visible*
You are so talented.	I felt respect for you when I heard you give the presentation.
You don't try hard enough.	I felt frustrated when I saw that you had read only part of the book.
You are so inconsiderate.	I felt disappointed when you didn't get me a ticket for the movie too.
You always embarrass me.	I felt embarrassed when you told everybody that I was taking swimming lessons.
You are such a funny guy.	I love the way you make me laugh.
You make it hard for me .	I feel nervous when you are looking over my shoulder. I find it hard to concentrate.
You never see a fault in anyone.	I admire your ability to see positive qualities in some people with whom I have real problems.

Notes for Sharing Directly

1. Start your statements with the word "I." The focus is on you, the speaker; therefore, use the pronoun "I."

2. Follow the words "**I feel**" with a feeling. You are sharing your feelings, so clearly state the emotion that you are experiencing.

    I feel *excited.*

    I feel *hurt.*

3. Connect the word "I" and the feeling with a perception of the other's behavior.

    Your feeling is connected to *a perception* that you are having. For example, you might feel excited when you *perceive* that your son is about to be elected to an office. At another time, you might feel hurt when you *perceive* that your friend is not paying attention to you. Thus your direct sharing would sound like this:

    I feel excited when it looks to me like you are going to be elected.

    And your direct sharing with your friend would sound like this:

    I felt hurt after school when you didn't seem to want to get together.

4. Use the word "when" to connect your feelings with your perception. You have feelings and perceptions at a specific time. Feelings and perceptions can change from moment to moment and from one experience to another. So use the word "when" to connect your feelings to your perceptions. For example,

    I felt impatient when you didn't seem to understand my instructions even after I repeated them.

5. Avoid saying the word "that" or "like" after saying "I feel." These words lead to judgments. For example,

"I feel that you are arrogant." "I feel like you don't care about others."

The phrases, *"You are arrogant"* and *"You don't care about others"* are judgments, not feelings.

Indirect Ways of Sharing: "Should Statements"

Like judgments, "should statements" that are directed towards another focus on that person and his or her behavior. Suppose a father tells his son, "You should study more." As the speaker of these words, the father's own feelings and needs are hidden. He might be experiencing one of the following:

♦ *anger* that his son is wasting time playing computer games.

♦ *concern* that his son is depressed and avoiding schoolwork.

♦ *sadness* that his son seems unmotivated as he was in high school.

He might be feeling many things and having many thoughts and needs. Very little of him is shared in the comment "You should study more." And probably very little of him will be heard by his son.

A father whose son had dropped out of college told us:

I was so angry with Roger, watching him wall himself up in his room. Periodically I'd get so fed up I'd give him a lecture on what he ought to be doing. He would get more sullen. We were going nowhere. Then I realized talking to my pastor how sad I felt seeing my son so unhappy and how helpless I felt to motivate him. I realized I didn't understand at all what he was feeling. The other night we had the best talk we've ever had. I told him how sad and helpless I felt. I told him that I wanted to listen to what he was thinking and feeling. We talked for over an hour—amazing. I think he really heard me and I think he felt that I listened.

Notice in the following that the "should statements" do not reveal the feelings of the speaker:

Should Statements	Direct Sharing
You should lose weight.	I feel afraid that you will pull your back out again like last year.
You should tell the doctor what you think.	I'm anxious that you will be frustrated about the treatment if you don't talk to her directly.
You should wait a year after your husband's death before moving.	I'm worried that you will regret your decision.
You should always greet people that way.	I felt proud of you when I saw you meet my new boss so warmly.
You should consider becoming a rabbi.	I admire the way you care for the people at temple.
You should have thought of that sooner.	I'm angry that we have to do this now.

Notes for Avoiding "Should Statements"

◆ Shift your focus from the other and onto yourself.

◆ Ask yourself, "What do I feel?"

◆ Then ask yourself, "What need or perception is the feeling connected to?"

◆ Avoid the word "should"!

We are all vulnerable and susceptible to any remark that threatens us, that sounds critical. Should statements that are directed at us tend to put us on the defensive. It is very hard to hear the speaker's care for us or respect for us when we are hearing "You should." It is very hard to understand what the speaker is experiencing at all. We hear about ourselves. We don't really hear the speaker. So, when you want to be heard, telling the other what he or she should do is a guaranteed means to thwart your own need.

Indirect Ways of Sharing: Speaking Impersonally

In our vulnerability we tend to protect ourselves by hiding behind our words. A French cynic quipped, "Words were invented to keep people from knowing one another." A common form of verbal subterfuge is use of the impersonal pronoun, "one." "*One* doesn't like to admit his mistakes." "*One* dreads tax time." The one in each of these cases is the speaker who is reluctant to say, "I don't like to admit my mistakes," or, "I dread tax time." Using the word "I" makes the speaker more exposed and therefore more vulnerable. The English commonly use "one" in this manner. The French have the word *on*. Americans tend to hide behind the word "we" or "you." "You don't want to tell other people what to do." "We all have a difficulty speaking up to authorities." By speaking in this way, an assertion, opinion, or feeling is made impersonal by implying that everyone feels the same way. It is a safe way of talking, but not very revelatory of the actual speaker. The impersonal pronoun is not much more than a fig leaf to cover our insecurity, but when we want to be heard even a small shield can get in the way. Notice that the impersonal pronoun hides the speaker in the following examples:

Impersonal Sharing	*Direct Sharing*
You don't want to be the spoilsport.	I'm afraid I'll ruin the party if I leave early.
We all have to pitch in get the job done.	I feel frustrated that you and have not finished your part of the project.
No one wants to be the first one to speak.	I'm anxious that I'll have to go first at the meeting.
One should keep things impersonal in the workplace.	I'm uncomfortable with revealing anything personal at work.
You would have to be crazy to travel now.	I'm afraid to travel now.

Notes for Speaking Personally

+ Avoid starting a statement with the words "we" or "you" or "one" if you really mean "I." These pronouns will direct your focus away from yourself.

+ Focus on your feeling. Attention to your feeling will direct your focus onto yourself and onto your personal experience.

◆ Be willing to reveal your own perception, feeling, or
   need.

Indirect Ways of Sharing:
Universal Expressions

More hiding of self occurs in universal expressions.
"Nobody likes a quitter." There might be some truth in the
expression, but if the remark comes from a mother whose
daughter wants to drop out of the drama club, it hides her
own feelings. She could be feeling impatient at her
daughter's change of mind, particularly when she has just
spent more money than she had wanted on costumes. She
might feel afraid of how her daughter's drama coach will
react. She might be concerned that she gives into her
daughter too easily. She could be experiencing a number of
feelings, but none are admitted in the phrase, "Nobody likes
a quitter," and probably none will be heard by her daughter.

"Everybody knows that women are more concerned
about their weight than men are." Whether "everybody"
does or doesn't have that view, it is probably the view of the
speaker. Maybe if he said, "I think that women are more
concerned about their weight than men are," he would feel
less secure and a bit more open to criticism. So "everybody
knows" replaces "I think." The universal remark might
solicit agreement or disagreement, but it won't invite
attentive listening to the personal feelings and views of the
speaker.

Universal or general expressions assert that all people or
all Americans or all businesses act or feel or think the same
way. Whether they do or do not, these statements tend to
keep the speaker from expressing his or her own personal
views. In general, they set off unresolveable arguments.
They imply "You *have* to agree with me." They substitute for

personal expressions and do little to invite intimate listening. Note how more direct and personal the direct sharing statements are than the universal expressions:

Universal Expressions	*Direct Sharing*
Everyone knows that voting is waste of time.	I think that my vote doesn't count.
No one wants to go to Human Resources with their issues.	I'm afraid to talk to anyone in Human Reources about my problems with my boss.
Don't bother trying to get a man to talk about his feelings.	I feel so disappointed when my husband says he doesn't feel anything.
People who have never been sick don't know what it is like to be in pain.	I'm fearful that I'll be seen as a whiner by people who are well.
Everyone in your family is so artistic.	I admire the way that you play the piano.

Notes for Avoiding Universal Expressions

♦ Take some time to reflect on why you are using the universal and not the more personal "I."

♦ If you want to be personal and intimate, then avoid statements that begin with "Everybody" or "No one."

- Learn to translate the impersonal, universal expressions into personal statements.

- Go back to the basic form of self-expression.

   Example: I felt (emotion) when I sensed that you (perception).

   Example: I felt sad when I sensed that you were going to drop out of our book club.

Indirect Ways of Sharing: Absolute Statements

Husband to Wife: You always talk too much at my parents' house.

Wife to Husband: You never show any affection for me.

These statements not only hide the speaker and his or her feelings, they strain credulity by allowing for no exceptions. "You always." "You never." It will be very difficult for the wife to hear what her husband might be feeling about visits to his parents while she is staving off his absolute "always." The husband will have just as hard a time hearing his wife's feelings and needs about affection while he is prompted to defend "never." *Absolute expressions tend to invite argument.* Exceptions to the "never" or "always" are produced and debated. The person uttering the absolute might be experiencing intense feelings that produce the no-exceptions complaint. But the absolute statement shatters any hope of being heard. Who will listen when subjected to criticism that is absolute? Consider the difference between absolute statements and direct personal expressions:

Absolute Statements	*Direct Sharing*
You never do the laundry.	I'm tired of being responsible for doing the laundry.
You always have to have the last word.	I feel hurt when you add a comment when I'm talking.
I'm always the one who has to be the disciplinarian in this house.	I resent it when I have to tell the children the curfew hour.
You always want to see sentimental movies.	I felt frustrated when you wouldn't consider going to the action movie I wanted to see.
We are never late for these sessions.	I feel proud of us when we're here on time.

Notes for Avoiding Absolute Statements

♦ If you start a statement with "You always . . ." or "You never . . . ," you are more than likely not going to be heard.

♦ To avoid the absolutes, identify *when* you felt the emotion.

♦ Resist using "always" or "never." A simple way to remember this suggestion is: always resist using "always" and never use "never."

Listen First If You Want to Be Heard

The surest way to invite listening behavior is to give it. You want and need your daughter to listen to you. Do you listen to her? Are you an example to her of a good listener? The golden rule of doing unto others as you would have them do unto you is wise. Why would your friend, brother, mother listen to you if they do not experience your attentive listening? Time and again in marriage counseling, we hear a spouse complain, "He [she] doesn't listen," and a minute later when his (her) spouse starts to talk the partner fails to listen, and instead objects, interrupts, or gives advice. A parent admitted to us recently,

> *I have been all over my sixteen-year-old about not listening to me. But when he told me that he didn't want to go on our family vacation to my parents' place, I went on and on about hurting his grandparents and why we need to be together as a family. I never once stopped to hear what he was feeling and thinking.*

Some parents have told us of their commitment to share their feelings at home so that the children grow up aware of and expressive of their emotions. The same goal could be set for listening. Children need to be heard. They also need to learn how to listen from their parents' example. If your partner or friend or employee doesn't listen to you, consider how well you listen to him or her. *It is easy to know when we are not heard. We can fail to notice, however, when we do not listen.* If the boss listens, there is a better chance that his managers will. If a husband listens, it is more likely that his wife will. You want to be heard—show the way to those whom you want to listen to you.

Most people would like to be good listeners, but they forget to listen. Habits of self-defense, me-too identifying, and advice giving are hard to break. When you want to be heard, it might be helpful before you talk to be direct about that need: "I need you to listen to me about . . . my day at work, or . . . what I felt toward my brother when he called." The process of learning to express yourself directly promotes both being heard and hearing the other. The more that you come to recognize your own impersonal expressions, the more expert and powerful you can become in hearing through the indirect expressions of others. So, while working to make it easier for someone to listen to you, you improve your ability to listen.

CHAPTER FIFTEEN

Concluding
Thoughts

They would not listen. They did not know how.

Perhaps they'll listen now.

—"Vincent" by Don McLean

Faithful reader, you have listened to us, the authors, through all of these pages. We ask you now to listen one final time. Listening is an essential behavior totally worth every effort to learn and to master. Listening takes us out of our tendency to self-absorption and self-protection. It opens us to the world around us and to the persons who matter most to us. When we listen, we learn, we grow, and we are nourished. We learn about those we care for by listening, by entering into them with genuine empathy. We learn to understand their feelings, their needs, their perspective, their view of themselves, their view of life, and their view of us. We grow tolerant of difference. We judge less and appreciate more. We are nourished as we listen— nourished by discovering more of the mystery and uniqueness of the individuals in our lives.

Travel has often been recommended for its ability to broaden our minds, to see that our culture, our customs, our values are not all that exists, that our way is not the only way and possibly not the best way. Listening is like traveling. We can enter the special, different "worlds" of those around us. We can grow to appreciate our child's unique rhythms, style, and interests. We can learn to cherish the little and big differences between ourselves and those we listen to respectfully—partners, spouses, colleagues, friends, and family members. Failure to understand cheats us of discovery and has devastating effects on the other. T. S. Eliot wrote,

Listening is like traveling. We can enter the special, different "worlds" of those around us.

> It is human, when we do not understand another human being and cannot ignore him, to exert an unconscious pressure on that person, to turn him into something that we can understand: many husbands and wives exert this pressure on each other. The effect on that person so influenced is liable to be repression and distortion, rather than improvement of the personality, and no man is good enough to have the right to make another over in his own image.

Each of us needs to be understood. In a conversation, being heard gives us the space to clarify our thoughts and to express our feelings. In a relationship, being heard frees us from isolation and unites us with the listener. When we are understood we become more able to know ourselves and then to accept ourselves. The greatest gift that we can receive from another person is pure attention, deep understanding. That attention allows us to be ourselves without fear and without shame.

We can give that pure attention, that careful listening to those individuals whose lives most touch ours: our spouse, partner, parent, child, sibling, friend, colleague, client, employee, boss. The gift demands discipline, putting ourselves aside or on "hold" for the moment. Such listening can be exhausting, but its rewards are great for the listener and for the one heard. As living beings we are meant to grow. Listening fosters growth in self-control, self-awareness, tolerance, and even wisdom. As human beings we are made to give life. When we listen attentively, lovingly, we liberate those whom we understand. We enable them to be themselves more freely. So learning to listen is not the mastering of a technique. It is, in essence, learning to love.

Reflection Questions

◉ Whom do you most want to really listen to you?

◉ What are the unsuccessful strategies or efforts you have used to obtain this person's attention and understanding?

◉ How can you practice sharing your feelings and needs directly?

Appendix One
Rules of Thumb for Listening

1. Make a commitment to listen to this person at this moment.

2. Do not act as though you are listening if your heart is not in it or if the time is not right for you to listen.

3. If you want to listen but are not free to pay attention at the moment, say so, but add that you would like to listen later. For example: "I can't give you my attention now, but how about we talk after I finish this report, say at 3:00?"

4. Focus on the speaker with your eyes and your body position.

5. Focus on the speaker's feelings, needs, and perceptions or on the information that is being communicated.

6. Register your own feeling and "hold it."

7. Be aware of your typical non-listening behaviors and try to control them.

8. Offer back what you are hearing in your own words with your voice rising in a questioning tone.

9. Don't presume that what you are hearing is exactly what the speaker is trying to say.

10. Don't stop listening after your first effort to express understanding. Keep listening until the speaker confirms that you have really understood.

Rules of Thumb for Being Heard

1. Start with the word "I." Sounds obvious, but watch how easy it is to slip into talking about the other person in the name of talking about yourself.

2. "I feel . . ." should be followed by a feeling. Be careful that "I feel . . ." is not followed by "that" or "you." When you start a statement with "I feel that . . ." or "I feel that you . . ." it usually becomes a judgment about the other person, not an expression of your feelings.

3. Be specific about time. Indicate when you felt the emotion. For example, "I felt delighted *this afternoon* when you walked into the room and smiled at me."

4. Connect the feeling and time to a perception. For example, "I felt nervous earlier when you asked me to come to your office. *You seemed tense.*"

5. When noting your perceptions, be sure to qualify them as *perceptions*, not facts. Use words such as *seems to me* or *appeared to me* or *looked like to me*. Perceptions are not facts. They reflect how things appear to you.

6. Don't share something important to you at a time or place that is not opportune. For example, don't initiate a tense conversation while your partner is watching his favorite television show or when your boss comes in first thing in the morning.

7. Don't use absolute statements such as, "You always . . ." or "You never . . ."

8. Don't use should statements such as, "You should be more spontaneous."

9. Don't judge: "You are too sensitive." "You're grouchy."

10. Don't speak impersonally if you want to be heard personally: *"One* doesn't like to be wrong." *"We* all need time to play."

11. Don't make generalizations: *"All women* like to talk." *"Men* don't share their feelings."

12. Listen to those whom you want to listen to you.

13. Keep the focus on you when admitting your feelings, needs, and perceptions.

14. Invite the one you want to hear you to listen. This may seem to go without saying, but if you don't alert your desired listener that you need to be heard, he or she may unwittingly forget to listen and instead turn the interaction into a debate, gripe session, or discussion about someone else.

Appendix Two

List of Feelings

adventurous
affectionate
afraid
agitated
alarmed
alert
alive
aloof
amazed
amused
angry
anguished
annoyed
anxious
apathetic
appreciative
aroused
ashamed
astonished
bewildered
bitter
blasé
blissful
bored
broken-hearted
buoyant
calm
carefree
cautious
cheerful
choked up
close
cold
comfortable

compassionate
complacent
composed
concerned
confident
confused
contemptuous
contented
cool
cooperative
courageous
cross
curious
deferential
defiant
dejected
delighted
dependent
depressed
despairing
despondent
detached
determined
disappointed
discouraged
disgruntled
disgusted
disheartened
dishonest
dismayed
dissatisfied
distant
distressed
disturbed

downcast
eager
ecstatic
edgy
effervescent
elated
electrified
embarrassed
embittered
encouraged
engrossed
enraged
enthusiastic
envious
estranged
evasive
exalted
exasperated
excited
exhilarated
expansive
exuberant
fascinated
fearful
fidgety
firm
forlorn
free
friendly
frightened
frisky
frustrated
furious
giddy

gloomy
good-humored
grateful
gratified
grieved
grumpy
guilty
gutless
happy
hard
heavy
helpful
helpless
hesitant
hopeful
hopeless
horrible
horrified
hostile
hot
humble
humdrum
hurt
immobilized
impatient
inadequate
independent
indifferent
infuriated
inquisitive
insecure
insensitive
inspired
intense
interested
intrigued
invigorated
involved
irate

irritated
jealous
jittery
joyful
jubilant
lonely
loving
mad
mean
melancholy
mellow
merry
mirthful
miserable
mixed-up
moved
open
optimistic
overwhelmed
panicky
paralyzed
peaceful
pessimistic
pleased
powerless
proud
puzzled
radiant
rancorous
rapturous
relieved
reluctant
repelled
resentful
respectful
restless
sad
satisfied
scared

secure
seductive
self-assured
sensitive
shaky
shocked
silly
skeptical
soft
sorry
sour
spiritless
startled
stimulated
submissive
suspicious
talkative
tense
terrified
thankful
thrilled
timid
torn
tranquil
troubled
trusting
uncomfortable
uneasy
unhappy
upset
uptight
warm
weepy
wide-awake
withdrawn
woeful
worried
wretched

Selected Bibliography

Berenson, Bernard G., and Robert R. Carkhuff. *Sources of Gain in Counseling and Psychotherapy.* New York: Holt, Rinehart and Winston, Inc., 1967.

Broyard, Anatole. "Doctor Talk to Me." *The New York Times Magazine* (August 26, 1990).

Craik, Dinah, an eighteenth-century poet

Donoghue, Paul J., and Mary E. Siegel. *Sick and Tired of Feeling Sick and Tired: Living With Invisible Chronic Illness.* New York: W.W. Norton and Company, 1992.

Eliot, T. S. "Notes Towards the Redefinition of Culture," part of the Memorial Lectures delivered at Yale University in 1970. The lecture is continued in *In Bluebeard's Castle: Some Notes Towards the Redefinition of Culture.* New Haven, Connecticut: Yale University Press, 1971.

Frankel, Richard M., M.D., and Howard Beckman. A study done at the University of Rochester Medical School in 1984.

James, Dan and Lilith James. *Bloomer Girl,* 1944 musical comedy.

Jourard, Sidney. *The Transparent Self.* New York: D. VanNostrand Company, 1971.

de Montaigne, Michel Eyquam. "Essais," as quoted by Gail Goodwin in *Mother and Two Daughters.* New York: Viking Press, 1982.

Richards, Mary Caroline. *Centering.* Middletown, Connecticut: Wesleyan Press, 1964.

Rilke, Rainer. *Letter to a Young Poet.* New York: W.W. Norton and Company, 1981.

Rogers, Carl R. Unpublished presentation of a talk given at the California Institute of Technology, Pasadena, California, November 9, 1964.

de Saint-Exupery, Antoine. *The Little Prince.* New York: Harcourt, Brace & World, Inc., 1943.

Schacter, Daniel. *The Seven Sins of Memory: How the Mind Forgets.* New York: Houghton, Mifflin and Company, 2001.

Shakespeare, William. *Hamlet.* New York: Washington Square Press, 2003.